A Guarded Life

A Guarded Life

My story of the dark side of An Garda Síochána

Majella Moynihan

with Aoife Kelleher

HACHETTE
BOOKS
IRELAND

First published in 2020 by Hachette Books Ireland

A CIP catalogue record for this title is available from the British Library.

ISBN 978 1 52933 598 9

Typeset in Sabon by redrattledesign.com

Printed and bound in Great Britain by
Clays Elcograf S.p.A

Hachette Books Ireland policy is to use papers that are natural, renewable
and recyclable products and made from wood grown in sustainable forests.
The logging and manufacturing processes are expected to conform to the
environmental regulations of the country of origin.

Hachette Books Ireland
8 Castlecourt Centre
Castleknock
Dublin 15, Ireland

A division of Hachette UK Ltd
Carmelite House, 50 Victoria Embankment, EC4Y 0DZ

www.hachettebooksireland.ie

Majella Moynihan was born in Kanturk, Co. Cork and raised in St. Joseph's Industrial School for Girls, Mallow. She served in An Garda Síochána for fifteen years, from 1983 to 1998. In 1984, she gave birth to a son, whom she was forced to give up for adoption, having been charged with breach of Garda disciplinary regulations for having sexual intercourse and giving birth outside of marriage. In 2019, on foot of an RTÉ Radio 1 documentary about her story, Majella received an official state apology. She lives in Dublin.

Aoife Kelleher is a journalist and filmmaker. Educated at Oxford University and the Dublin Institute of Technology, she has made many award-winning documentaries, including *One Million Dubliners*, *We Need To Talk About Dad* and, in 2019, *The Case of Majella Moynihan*. *A Guarded Life* is her first book.

Contents

For David and Stephen

'We realise the importance of our voice
when we are silenced.'
– Malala Yousafzai

'No matter where we live on the planet
or how difficult our situation seems to be,
we have the ability to overcome and
transcend our circumstances.'
– Louise Hay

Prologue

The 29th of September, 1983, should have been the best day of my life. That was the day I graduated from the Garda Training College in Templemore, County Tipperary and officially became a member of An Garda Síochána.

It was the fulfilment of a lifelong dream. As a young girl, growing up in an orphanage – St. Joseph's Industrial School in Mallow – I can remember telling the other girls that I was going to be a guard and look after the vulnerable in society, especially the forgotten little children. Forgotten little children like we were, then.

Even by the 1970s, when I was in school, joining 'the guards' was still an unusual career choice for a young woman in Ireland. Women had only been admitted to the police force in 1959 and the numbers of banghardaí, as they were called then, were still very low. I had never seen a female guard but I knew they were out there and the job held a special appeal for me.

I thought I could bring something very different to the role. Having lost my mother as an infant and then been placed in the orphanage by my father, I knew what it was to suffer; I knew what isolation was and I knew the pain of being different. I knew what could happen to someone to lead them to commit a crime. I knew what could break a person because I was broken myself. On the other hand, I knew we all had choices in this world and that, if you made the choice to commit a crime, you had to be brought to justice.

To me, An Garda Síochána was the ultimate symbol of justice. As a child in an industrial school, you quickly learned that the world wasn't a fair place but, in spite of suffering years of abuse and neglect, I had retained my strong sense of justice. I believed that joining the force would mean that, in my own small way, I would have a chance to right some of the wrongs that were done to people every day.

Of course, there was a bit of ego there too. A motherless 'St. Joseph's girl', as they called us in Mallow, becoming a guard? By any standards, that was some achievement. We had had civil servants and nurses in our family but we had never had a bangharda and I hoped my mam would be looking down on me that day with pride.

My stepmother, Kitty, was coming down for my graduation and passing-out parade, the traditional ceremony for recruits who had completed their training. She had told me not to expect my father – it was, after all, a long train journey from Dublin, she explained, and at fifty-eight years old, he felt he was past the time in his life for making long journeys. I was hurt at the prospect of his absence. I had spent so little time with my father over the years – I was only one year old when he sent me and my sisters away to be raised by the nuns. Our relationship had never been warm and yet I was still desperate for his love and approval. If he wasn't going to come to Templemore, I hoped that, wherever he was, he was pleased at what his youngest daughter had accomplished.

When I woke that morning, I was cheerful in the knowledge that I had set myself on the right path. I felt that I now had everything I needed to fulfil my potential and live a good, successful and happy life. In front of me, hanging on the wardrobe door, were the two outfits I would wear that day – my garda uniform and the grown-up grey suit I had chosen for the evening festivities. The previous week, the other girls and I had tried on our outfits together, full of excitement, scarcely able to believe that we had made it through training and were now just days away from becoming banghardaí.

Of the eighteen recruits in my class, six of us were women. If we had harboured any illusions that we would be regarded as just as good as the men, our time in Templemore had made it clear that, in the training college at least, that would not be the case. From the moment we arrived and were given skirts and heels as part of our uniform, we were treated differently by almost all the senior guards. It was implied that we were mainly there to help with cases of rape and domestic violence and other so-called 'women's issues'. Only one sergeant, Dan Corrigan, told us we could be anything we wanted to be. I remember looking around as he said those words and seeing on the faces of the other women that this affirmation meant as much to them as it did to me.

The passing-out ceremony was due to begin at twelve noon, and by 10 a.m. families and friends had already begun to arrive. The minister of state at the Department of Justice and the garda commissioner would be inspecting us and there were rumours that there might even be television cameras from RTÉ News. I sat at my window in a state of nervous anticipation, already wearing my full uniform. As well as my stepmother and her sisters, my boyfriend Fintan was also due to attend the ceremony and I was hoping he might come early. There was something I needed to tell him.

Fintan was himself a newly qualified guard. We had met at the Garda Club on Harrington Street in Dublin the previous year, a matter of months before he left for Templemore. Fintan had passed out in May and was now stationed in County Donegal, a five-hour drive from Templemore, so, when we met up at weekends, it was usually in Dublin.

Fintan would be outside by now. Standing away from my stepmother, whom he hardly knew. It was time for me to head out too. I took one last look in the mirror, smoothed out my navy-blue tunic over my reassuringly flat stomach, put on my hat and off I went. Soon to be Bangharda Number 338 of 339 in An Garda Síochána...

That night, after the hat throwing and the dinner, I finally plucked up the courage and took Fintan aside. 'I think I'm in trouble,' I told him. 'My period is three days late. This has never happened to me before and I'm worried that I could be pregnant.'

The last time we had been together, Fintan had stayed over at our family home in Phibsborough. We had slept together but, unusually, Fintan didn't have any condoms. Hearing my suspicions, Fintan appeared unfazed by my concerns, assuring me that everything would be grand.

But it wasn't nothing. It was *something*. And, before long, that little something would bring the wrath of An Garda Síochána down upon my head.

1

Losing Mammy

Many years before I even considered joining An Garda Síochána, the course my life was to take was set on the morning of 2 January 1964, when my mother died.

I had been born only eighteen months previously, on 10 June 1962, the fifth of five daughters, to Hugh and Margaret Moynihan. We lived on a little farm in the townland of Fermoyle, three miles south of Banteer, in north County Cork. My father himself came from Fermoyle and he had two sisters and a brother living close by.

To this day, I know little about my mother, who was one of twelve siblings and came from a village on the Cork–Kerry border called Knocknagree. From what I have been told over the years, she was an attractive and fun-loving woman, with a warm, playful laugh and short black hair. She was a homemaker, who baked and raised her children and, at the weekends, she loved to dance. She and my father used to waltz and jive at dance competitions all around north Cork and I have heard that they danced beautifully together.

She always insisted on going into Mallow and Kanturk and buying beautiful new outfits for her five girls. Because I had no memories of Mammy myself, I always loved hearing about the care she took in dressing me and my sisters. Any evidence at all that I had once had a mother who loved me was very precious indeed.

Hugh Moynihan was tall and well-built. He was a good-looking man, who always took pride in his appearance. My older sisters tell me that, before Mammy died and we were put into care, he was a kind and devoted father, who always had time for his family and used to make wooden toys and wheelbarrows for the girls when they were young. Although we had the farm, Dad made most of his money working as a contractor. He owned a combine harvester and used to travel around north Cork, cutting corn on the bigger farms. He was never afraid of work, my father, and I'm sure that, if we had stayed with him, we would have had a very comfortable life.

After I was born, my mother developed post-natal depression and was put into a hospital in Cork city.

My father struggled to cope with raising five daughters on his own and, in June 1963, my four sisters were put into an orphanage, St. Joseph's Industrial School for Girls in Mallow. Catherine was ten years old, Anne was nine, Margaret was six and Teresa was four.

On the day the girls were taken away, one of our cousins told them that they were to come for a drive in his car. Only my sister Anne noticed the brown suitcase in the front seat and asked where they were going. The man said nothing, but kept driving until they got to Mallow. When they arrived at St. Joseph's, the four girls were handed over to a nun at the door.

I was still only a baby, so I stayed with my Auntie Mary, Mammy's sister, until 10 December 1963 when, at eighteen months old, I too was brought to the orphanage. Unlike my sisters, who slept in one of the four dormitories in St. Joseph's, I stayed with the other babies in the infirmary. Mammy was doing much better by then and it was expected that we would only stay in the orphanage for another few weeks. On 2 January, the brown suitcase was packed and we were ready to go, when a call came through to St. Joseph's to say that Mammy was dead.

Years later, I was told that my mother had cycled to Barracarrig to visit our Auntie Mary. When she left to go home, my cousin Tom Twomey walked with her to the end of the boreen and waved her off. A short time later, the Twomeys heard that someone had been knocked off a bike on the main road and killed. When they came out to investigate, they realised it was Mammy.

Her death was what would now be described as a 'hit and run'. There were no witnesses and no one ever came forward to say it was their vehicle that had killed her. Because we were just children, my sisters and I were never told any of the details of how she died. All we heard was people saying, 'Wasn't it awful sad about the Moynihans' mother?' We didn't attend the funeral; we stayed in St. Joseph's, where we would each remain until we finished school.

Shortly after my mother's death, my father went to England, never to return to live in Cork.

2

A St. Joseph's girl

My earliest memory is of starting school in Coláiste Íosagáin Infant School in Mallow. I was a skinny little girl, small for my age, with big green eyes and long dark hair, like a doll. I remember on the first day how the other children all had their mammies with them to put on their slippers and hang up their coats, things I had to do by myself. I felt that everyone could see right away that I was different. When things were hard for the other children or when they did well, they had someone to help them or to celebrate with them. From a young age, I longed for what they had.

Instead of a mammy, I had Sr. Claire Caplice, from Kildorrery, County Cork, a warm woman who was the head of St. Joseph's, and Nellie O'Brien, a lay woman, who was Sr. Claire's second-in-command. Both Sr. Claire and Nellie lived in quarters in St. Joseph's, along with Mary, who worked in the laundry and Patsy the cook, and together they ran the orphanage. Sr. Claire was a big, tall woman with the happiest face you could imagine. She was maternal with all the girls and especially so with me and three of my friends: Elizabeth O'Callaghan, whom everybody called Betty, and the two little blonde sisters, Marguerite and Marie Murphy. We had all come into the orphanage as babies and I think that that was the reason Sr. Claire had a soft spot for us. Betty's story was very similar to mine. Like me, she had been brought to St. Joseph's when she was just a year old, after her mother died. Her father was still living but, unlike my own father, Betty's often came to visit her or to bring her out for the day. Both of Marguerite and Marie's parents were alive but their mother was very ill – too sick to take care of the girls – so they, too, had been left at St. Joseph's.

The four of us became known as 'Sr. Claire's girls' and she was very protective of us. She could not have shown us any more love than she did. Every so often, she'd turn to one of us and say, 'Oh, you're a beautiful little girl!' or some other kind words like that, and since we were longing for tenderness and attention, we used to follow her around to hear them all the time.

Sr. Claire managed St. Joseph's with calm authority. If there was a decision to be made, she was the one to make it. She spent most of the day in her office, doing the books; then she'd have dinner with the other nuns in the convent and, in the evening, she'd come back to St. Joseph's and she and Nellie would have friends come to visit. They'd sit in the kitchen, laughing and making tea and toast. As soon as we heard the laughter and smelled the food, we'd hang around the door like lost souls, begging for some toast, but we never got any! For the most part, though, Sr. Claire was very generous. She had a contact in the chocolate factory, which was up in the town, who used to send all of the broken chocolate to the orphanage. We called it chocolate crumb and it was our favourite treat. As soon as it arrived, Sr. Claire would give it out – she wouldn't wait for Sunday or a feast day. She never hoarded anything – it was one of the many things I loved about her.

The years when Sr. Claire was in charge were the happiest of my childhood. Her warmth and good nature made the absence of my mother easier to bear and her kindness made me feel accepted and cared for. I had an overwhelming need for affection as a child because it was a talisman against my deepest fear, which was that I was unlovable. After all, if I had been lovable, surely my father wouldn't have sent me away.

St. Joseph's Industrial School for Girls was under the auspices of the Sisters of Mercy and could accommodate up to eighty children, though there might normally have been fifty or sixty in residence at any given time. We shared a campus with St. Mary's Convent, a large, looming, three-storey building, the main structure of which was Gothic Revival and dated back to 1860, though multiple extensions had since been added. From the outside, St. Joseph's looked like a big, grey house, but the large statue of St. Joseph on the lawn was a reminder that this was a religious institution. I always felt as though I was walking into a jail whenever I passed through the front door, which was not a regular occurrence, as the main entrance was reserved for nuns and guests. Girls were supposed to go in around the back.

The day ran to a strict schedule: up in the morning for mass, then chores and helping to clean the convent, then breakfast and off to school; we came back for dinner and wash-up, then back to school for the afternoon classes. In the evening, we had a cup of cocoa with bread and jam, then it was music or dance practice, followed by homework with Nellie. Sometimes we were allowed to watch a little bit of television before prayers in the landing and bed.

For the little girls, there was a playground, with swings, a merry-go-round, an ocean wave and see-saws. While the older girls did chores, we could run around or play shop or marbles or push each other on the swings. Our favourite game of all was one we played with five stones, called 'Gobs'. Each player had to throw up a stone with one hand and, while the stone was in the air, pick up the other four stones with the same hand. It sounds very basic – and it was – but we never seemed to tire of it.

In those early years, I shared a dormitory with Betty, Marguerite and Marie. In bed at night, after lights out, we'd each call out 'Goodnight' to one another – unless one of us was fighting with someone and then it would be 'Goodnight to everyone except the one in the corner!' After the goodnight routine, it was straight to sleep.

Our music and dance classes were of a very high standard. It wasn't just one of the nuns from the convent instructing us in hymns, we had a proper music teacher, Sylvia Nagle, who came in to teach us singing. The girls who took dance classes were taught Irish dancing by a dance teacher, Mrs Aldritch. I never liked dancing but I liked singing and I sang solo and took part in the choir. St. Joseph's was known throughout Cork for singing and dancing and Sr. Claire and Nellie were very proud of our accomplishments. We competed every year in the Cork County Scór na nÓg, where we were up against choirs, singers and dance troupes from all over the county, not just from other industrial schools and orphanages. I won the solo singing competition in 1977, singing the Irish song 'Trasna na dTonnta'.

On Saturday we went to confession. Every single week, as soon as we were old enough to start school, we would walk through the town to St. Mary's church in Mallow to tell our sins to the parish priest or the monsignor. We hardly knew, at that age, what a sin was. Betty, Marguerite, Marie and I would walk together, and on the way we would decide among ourselves what we should confess to. It was almost always some variation on the theme of 'I told lies, I was bold and I was late for mass.' The priest must have rolled his eyes when he saw us coming. As we walked back up Fair Street to St. Joseph's, you'd often hear people say to each other, 'Look at the orphans.' I always wanted to stop and tell them, 'I'm not an orphan, I have a daddy,' but I knew the next question would be 'Well, where is he, then?' and it wasn't much of an answer to say he was in England, so I said nothing.

On Saturday night, if the older girls had finished all their chores, we were allowed to watch television in the study hall. We all sat on the floor, the little ones up at the front. Sometimes, if there was a film on, the nuns would come over from the convent and we would get sweets and a packet of crisps. The first film I ever saw in the school gym hall is still my favourite one to this day – *The Sound of Music*. I'll never forget what a magical experience it was to watch it as a little girl growing up in the grounds of a convent. Naturally, I imagined myself as Maria and Sr. Claire as the kind reverend mother. The idea that a girl from an austere, regimented background, just like mine, could grow up to meet a handsome man and spend her time singing and raising children was the most wonderful thing I could imagine. The Mercy nuns loved it too – especially when the Benedictine sisters helped the Von Trapps to escape from the Nazis.

On Sundays we had visits. My sisters and I had quite a lot of visitors as my father's sisters often came to see us, and occasionally my father's brothers. Sometimes cousins would come and, once or twice a year, we went out to Fermoyle to visit my father's family. If Sr. Claire knew there were people coming, we would have to have a bath and get dressed up in our best clothes and, when the visitors came, we had to sing and dance for them, to show off the great education we were getting in the orphanage. I never had any time for visitors. I didn't want to see them and I certainly didn't want to perform for them. What were they doing coming to visit us in St. Joseph's? Why weren't we living with them? I couldn't understand how somebody could come into an orphanage and see five little girls being raised in there, only to walk out the door and relinquish all responsibility for them. Years later, I was told that it had been my father's preference to keep us together in the industrial school, instead of dividing us out among willing relatives.

Visits were the one occasion when my sisters and I spent time together as a family. A shout would go up: 'There's someone here to see the Moynihans!' and all five of us would come running from different parts of the orphanage and converge on the parlour, where we would take turns performing our song and dance routines. My usual party piece was 'The Irish Soldier Laddie':

> *It was a morning in July, I was walking through*
> *Tipperary*
> *When I heard a battle cry from the mountains*
> *overhead*
> *As I looked up in the sky I saw an Irish soldier*
> *laddie*
> *He looked at me right fearlessly and said:*
> *'Will you stand in the band like a true Irish man,*
> *And go and fight the forces of the crown?*
> *Will ye march with O'Neill to an Irish battle field?*
> *For tonight we go to free old Wexford town!'*

That done, we would disperse and return to our own groups of friends, our chores and games of Gobs. We never lived like a family of sisters and no effort was ever made by anyone to help us to become close. In reality, I hardly knew them, apart from Catherine who, as the eldest, looked out for me and made sure that I had clothes and was given my equal share when Daddy sent money down.

At Christmastime, Santa would come to the orphanage and all the nuns would be brought over from the convent to watch as we opened the presents that had been donated by the Lions Club in Mallow. The nuns, the Lions Club and the good people of Mallow looked on as we played with our handouts. I would feel sick in my tummy as we were put on display, knowing to show the appropriate amount of gratitude for the charity we were receiving. I decided then that I hated Santy and anybody else who insisted on giving me something for nothing.

Still, Christmas wasn't all bad. Each December, until she retired, Sr. Claire brought us to the Opera House in Cork for the pantomime. I still remember travelling up with the other girls at the back of the bus to Cork city, in our element. We'd file into the theatre in twos and Sr. Claire would get us ice cream and crisps and a bottle of Stripe. The shows were brilliant – every year, no matter what the story was, the famous Cork comedian and pantomime legend Billa O'Connell would play the dame or 'the granny'. I loved it.

The high point of the year in St. Joseph's was the feast day of St. Joseph, on 19 March. We used to have a party, with sweets and cans of Appla and 'fatty fats', which were like teacakes, with chocolate-covered marshmallow, and the pièce de résistance was a huge baked Alaska for dessert. You can imagine how wonderful it all was for the eighty little girls living in an orphanage, where the usual diet consisted of lumpy porridge for breakfast and mutton for dinner.

One Sunday, in 1969, my sisters and I were told to put on our very best dresses because we were going to have a special visit. When we walked into the parlour, our father was sitting there. He announced to the five of us that he had come home from England for good. He paused then and I wondered if he was about to ask us to live with him, now that he was back in Ireland. Instead, he told us that there was someone he wanted us to meet. An elegant lady, with light brown hair and a slim figure, walked into the room. She shook our hands and told us her name was Kitty. My father said that he and Kitty had been married for a full year. They had met in England, though Kitty was from Cork, like ourselves. Kitty and my father were going to live in Dublin and we would be able to come and see them as soon as they moved into their new house, on Shandon Road in Phibsborough.

It was not lost on me that my father's living arrangements with his new wife didn't include his children, and it was something I would grapple with for many years, and never fully understand. Perhaps something changed in him after my mother died and, in his grief, he justified to himself his abandonment of his daughters. As the youngest, I had no memory of anything other than institutional life, yet there was always a piece of me that yearned for a proper home, with a mother and father. For whatever reason, it was never to be.

To give my father his due, he sent us money every week, without exception. We were one of the families in the orphanage that the other children envied because we had the best of everything – clothes, shoes, whatever we needed. Our new stepmother Kitty also began to send us parcels. But while on a material level, I wanted for nothing, I was starved of the one thing I really needed, which was love.

Although my father didn't take us out of the orphanage after his return to Ireland, he did take the five of us for a few days during the summer holidays every year. We never went away to the seaside or anything like that, because my father was always busy with work, but we all stayed together in the house in Phibsborough. Kitty used to give us money to go shopping in town or to go to the cinema and, in the evenings, she'd bring home cakes and chocolates from the supermarket where she worked. Although it was nice to have a break, it was very difficult for us to see our father getting on with his life up in Dublin, knowing that we would soon be returning to the industrial school in Mallow.

Having never spent much time with my sisters at the orphanage, on these short holidays I got to know their personalities. Catherine, the eldest, was very kind and maternal; Anne, who came next, was more extroverted. Margaret was quieter and more gentle and Teresa was great fun – always chatting and laughing.

In my letters home, I had started to refer to Kitty and my father as 'Mammy and Daddy'. I had never had a mammy before and it gave me a little thrill every time I used the word. But one day, when I was staying in Shandon Road, I called Kitty 'Mammy' to her face, and she turned away from me and said, 'I am not your mother.' I was heartbroken. Kitty wasn't a venomous person and I don't believe there was any malice in what she said – I think she was just trying to make her position clear – but her words were a lash to a lonely child.

Thank goodness for Sr. Claire. She couldn't make up for the absence of my mother – she had too many children clamouring for her attention to be able to give us all the love we needed and the little pats she gave us on our heads were no substitute for a maternal embrace – but as long as she was around, things were never as bad as they might have been. I would have done anything for her. As we got older, Betty, Marguerite, Marie and I used to vie for her attention, taking on jobs like bringing up her hot water bottle and laying it out on her bed or leaving her lemon drink on the nightstand. We loved her. Sr. Claire remains the kindest woman I have ever known.

In school, I was known as 'Majella Moynihan, St. Joseph's girl' and although I was never treated differently by the other pupils, I was definitely treated differently by the staff. I felt that my status gave them, and especially the nuns, permission to say and do what they liked. First class was very tough. By then, I was in the convent primary school and my teacher was Sr. Josephine. She often singled me out for punishment. On one occasion, someone in the class farted very loudly and she decided that I was the culprit. 'Majella Moynihan,' she said, 'come up here!' and she made me stand in front of everyone. There was a piano in her classroom and she brought me behind it and pulled down my knickers. She said out loud, 'It wasn't you', and then she sent me back to my desk. I remember, at seven years old, forcing back the tears, trying desperately to hide my humiliation and shame.

That was the year I made my First Holy Communion. Nellie went searching in the store room and found a dress for me to wear. It was short, just to my knees, and even though it was a hand-me-down, I felt wonderful in it. I thought that I looked like a fairy.

Two Sundays before my communion, I got a visit from Nora Coakley, a former St. Joseph's girl who had always been particularly kind to me. The older girls often came back for visits to see the little ones and bring them sweets and presents. That day, Nora brought me a prayer book, a set of white rosary beads and a little white bag to go with my communion dress. Nellie must have written to tell her that I didn't have any of my own. I couldn't believe it. I think I gave Nora five hugs and at least a dozen kisses. It was one of the best presents I have ever received.

The night before the ceremony, all of the communicants had a bath and then Nellie came to our bedrooms and tied nylons in our hair, so we would have ringlets the following day. We had never been made to feel so important in our lives! I had convinced myself that my father and stepmother would come down to Mallow to see me so, in the morning, I got dressed as fast as I could and ran downstairs to await their arrival. A little group had already formed in the hall, where Nellie was calling out the names of the girls whose families had come to collect them. I watched as, one by one, girls had their veils adjusted or their dresses admired by smiling relatives, who then walked or drove them to the church. The ceremony was due to begin at 10.30 a.m. and by 9.45 all the other girls had been collected. Nellie told me we would have to leave or miss the mass entirely. 'Five more minutes,' I begged her, and ran to the window to keep a lookout. At 9.50, when they still hadn't arrived, Nellie pinched my cheek and said, 'Never mind, Majella. We'll send them a photo.' Then she called my sister Catherine and asked her to walk me over to St. Mary's church.

After the ceremony, all the girls mingled together in the churchyard, showing off their hair and outfits. I was one of the few children who didn't have any family there, which aroused a great deal of sympathy among the parents who attended. As a result, I got a great haul of communion money – £21! Mrs Murphy

– Marguerite and Marie's mother – was particularly generous and told me that I looked like a princess. I treasured that compliment for years afterwards. Nellie called out to us to be back in time for dinner, as Catherine took my hand and brought me into Mallow. When we got to the corner shop in Fair Street, she bought me the biggest ice-cream cone I had ever seen. It was a miracle it didn't end up all over my dress!

3

Rule of the iron fist

One evening in 1975, when I was twelve years old and in sixth class in primary school, Sr. Claire gathered all the girls together and told us she had reached the age of retirement and would be moving out of St. Joseph's and going to live in the convent with the rest of the Mercy sisters. We were devastated and begged her to stay but Sr. Claire told us not to worry, that we would still see her all the time and that there was a lovely nun coming to replace her.

The following week, we were introduced to Sr. Agnes. She gave a grand speech as we assembled outside the kitchen, and told us that, from now on, we would be getting pocket money every week and would be allowed to go to the pictures. This announcement was met with a flurry of excitement, as a group of girls whose social lives had hitherto been extremely limited imagined themselves mixing with the other children of Mallow, frequenting the cinema and buying all the sweets they could eat.

But the positivity and elation initially aroused by this new era at St. Joseph's was not to last. After a few weeks, it became clear that the promised pocket money and cinema trips would not materialise but, by then, that was the least of our troubles. Sr. Agnes had set about dismantling and removing every last vestige of Sr. Claire's time in St. Joseph's. She had Nellie and Mary the laundry woman moved to a bungalow on the grounds and replaced them with a nun called Sr. Concepta and a lay woman called Caroline. Under this new administration, the real hardship began.

Looking back, it must have been hard for Sr. Agnes to take over an institution where her predecessor, Sr. Claire, had been so adored. The older girls, myself included, felt that no new nun had a right to tell us what to do and we treated her arrival and the changes she was making with a certain amount of haughtiness and resentment. No doubt it was challenging for her: for most of us, Sr. Claire was the closest thing to a parent we'd ever known. It was to be expected that her departure from St. Joseph's would be a wrench. But Sr. Agnes showed little leniency. She was hard on us all and seemed to take a particular dislike to 'Sr.

Claire's girls'. Of that little group, I stood out as the most outspoken and cheeky. If I failed to comply with a request, or showed even a moment's hesitation, I would get a slap.

Sr. Agnes had a keen eye for insecurities. Girls who had living parents were told that if their mothers or fathers were any good, they wouldn't be living in St. Joseph's. By contrast, any orphaned girl who crossed her path was lucky to have been taken in by the Sisters of Mercy and not 'left to die in the street'. The insult Sr. Agnes selected for me was 'good-for-nothing'. It was a phrase that she hurled whenever she caught sight of me and these were often the last words I heard before I went to sleep at night.

Sr. Agnes's arrival coincided with the beginning of my time in St. Mary's Secondary School, and the resulting decline in my mood and behaviour began to have an impact at school as well. Sr. Agnes often kept me up after the other girls had gone to bed for punishment, so I was tired and unfocused during the day and was rarely ever given the chance to open a book in the evenings. My grades were atrocious, my self-esteem in tatters.

By second year, I had developed an eating disorder. I wanted somebody to realise how unhappy I was and I felt that, if I stopped eating, they might see it. I quickly lost a stone and a half and, though I had always been skinny, I now looked gaunt. Sr. Agnes took my illness as a personal affront. She brought me to Dr. O'Meara in Mallow and told him that I was refusing to eat because I was looking for notice. While I was vomiting in the toilet, she would wait outside the door and slap me in the face when I came out. In the morning, while all the other girls went off to school, she would stand over me and try to force me to eat my porridge. I would sit in front of the bowl without eating a morsel, and only at nine o'clock, when it was time for her own working day to begin, would she give up and tell me to go to school. I was late almost every day.

The years with Sr. Agnes were very hard for everyone in St. Joseph's. Our Christmas trips to the pantomime, our film nights with the nuns and any other little treats which we had enjoyed were cancelled. Any privacy we had become accustomed to with Sr. Claire disappeared, as, even though we now had single rooms, Sr. Agnes would descend on us at all hours of the day or night to check on our behaviour. If she left the orphanage for a few hours to run an errand or visit her family, she would send Sr. Concepta or Caroline around to spy on us and report back to her. Marie made up a song about the three of them:

> *Fuck them all, fuck them all*
> *The long and the short and the small*
> *First Concepta, then Caroline:*
> *they're stubborn and brazen*

But Agnes is the worst of them all.

We sang it on the way to school or hummed it to ourselves as we did our chores. We each, now, had new cleaning jobs to do in the orphanage or in the convent in the morning before school. I had to clean the cloisters, where the nuns would walk. The Mercy sisters would greet me and wish me good morning as I worked and I would just grimace back at them because I felt so aggrieved.

Every weekend, Marguerite, Marie, Betty and I would go to visit Sr. Claire. We often complained to her about Sr. Agnes and described the bullying we were subjected to. Sr. Claire always listened sympathetically but it was clear there wasn't much she could do. Sr. Agnes was the boss now and she made certain that everyone knew it.

One of the worst beatings she ever gave me – and the one that did the most lasting damage – happened when I was fifteen years old. In Inter Cert year, we had regular supervised study sessions with a nun from the convent, Sr. Gertrude, and one evening I was late coming down. Sr. Gertrude and Sr. Agnes took me across the corridor to the room we called 'The Playroom' and Sr. Agnes asked why I was late. I told her to leave me alone and she flew into a rage at once. When this happened, she would go pale with anger. While Sr. Gertrude was scolding me for being so cheeky, Sr. Agnes screamed that I was a stupid good-for-nothing, adding that if anyone needed to be early for study, it was me. Next she grabbed me by the hair and banged my head four times against the radiator. My eardrum was damaged that day, which I'm convinced led to the repeated ear infections I suffered afterwards.

By the end of the year, I was depressed and thin and so anxious I could barely string a sentence together. It was a surprise to nobody when I failed my Inter Cert, which was more ammunition for Sr. Agnes, who could now add 'idiot' and 'dunce' to the list of names she had for me.

I realised that I was either going to allow my spirit to be broken in its entirety by Sr. Agnes or I was going to have to rebel. I decided on the latter. My first act focused on Sr. Agnes's cranky henchwoman, Sr. Concepta. She was giving out to me one day, bossing me around and telling me what to do and it suddenly occurred to me that I was much taller than she was, so I told her that if she didn't shut up, I'd burst her! Of course Sr. Concepta told Sr. Agnes, who told me that I wasn't to speak to Sr. Concepta or anyone like that again. I said, 'I'll speak whatever way I want to' and braced myself for Sr. Agnes's response. But there was none. She glared at me and told me to get out of her sight but, remarkably, there was no beating or punishment. I still don't know why I escaped so lightly that day. It was a mistake on Sr. Agnes's part because it emboldened me to stand up for myself more often and to seek out other forms of mischief, as my teenage rebellion took wings.

4

First love

For the girls of St. Joseph's, our friends and classmates who were day pupils at St. Mary's Secondary School were our windows to the outside world. I used to look forward to going to school, not for the joy of being educated so much as for the relief of feeling that I was part of civilisation. The day girls taught us about fashion and make-up, they brought in magazines like *Jackie* and told us about the latest pop music. Through them, we got a sense of what ordinary life was like in Mallow – the kind of life where a sixteen-year-old girl could go where she wanted, do as she pleased and befriend whomsoever she chose. We were particularly interested in the fact that they knew boys – not just brothers and cousins and uncles, like the ones who might come to visit us in the orphanage, but mysterious boys from up the town who were related to nobody we knew and got up to God-knows-what in their spare time.

To say that fraternising with boys like that would be frowned upon at St. Joseph's would be an understatement of considerable proportions. We were being raised by nuns with a view to, if not becoming nuns ourselves, then at least behaving like them. We were still attending mass every day, confession once a week and also benediction on a Sunday evening, to which women, including ourselves, wore black mantillas to cover their hair, while the priest walked around the church with a monstrance, blessing us all with the Eucharist.

We had no sex education whatsoever. No one ever sat down with us and told us about puberty and how it would change your body and nobody said anything to us about periods. Through the older girls, we learned about using rags and how to pin them to our underwear. No one in St. Joseph's had ever officially had a boyfriend and, certainly, no boy who wasn't a relative had ever come to call on any girl there.

One day, as we were walking between classes in St. Mary's, a friend of mine, Ciara Willis, divulged that one of the local boys, Shane O'Connor, had told her he fancied me. I couldn't believe it. 'Shane O'Connor?' I said. 'He's gorgeous!' Shane O'Connor was more than gorgeous. At six foot four, he was literally head and shoulders above most of the other boys in Mallow and, with his brown eyes and dark hair, his looks were the stuff that teenage girls' dreams were made of.

I arranged with Ciara and some of the other day girls to tell Shane and his friends that we'd meet them at the chipper at nine o'clock. It was then just a matter of sneaking out of St. Joseph's at the appointed time. The doors were rarely locked until after ten, to facilitate Sr. Agnes and Sr. Concepta's comings and goings between the orphanage and the convent, but I couldn't run the risk of meeting either one of them on my route. At a quarter to nine, I crept down to the dressing room, where there was a small hatch, leading to a laundry chute where we threw our dirty clothes. I climbed into the hatch, went down the chute and came out in the empty laundry room, where an unlocked door opened onto the convent farm. From there, it was just a quick walk through the grounds, through a side gate and out into Mallow.

Mallow in 1978 was really just one big main street but to me it seemed like the most exciting place in the world. I had only ever seen snatches of it when we went to mass or to the doctor or dentist, or when I was chosen to go to the Monument House supermarket to get messages for the nuns or to collect their prescriptions from O'Sullivan's chemist.

The hour I spent in the town that evening was

nothing less than magical. I met Ciara and the girls and we shared a few cigarettes before the lads arrived and insisted on paying for our chips. Then we walked around, eating and talking and smoking. I felt fantastic strolling along with Shane and, what's more, for the first time ever I felt normal, as though I was just another one of the day girls, with a family and a social life and a boyfriend.

Shane was curious about life in St. Joseph's and asked about our rooms and where we all ate and who came to visit us and what we did at weekends. For the day girls, this was old news – we had been friends for years and had been over the subject of life in an orphanage many times before – so they left us to our conversation. The last thing I wanted to talk about was St. Joseph's and its dormitories and refectory but I answered all of Shane's questions, while glossing over the parts of my life that caused me the most embarrassment and pain.

Shane walked me back to St. Joseph's gate and gave me a kiss on the cheek before I went in. I was so delighted, I practically skipped through the grounds and up to the laundry door – but all of my joy evaporated when I tried it and found that it was locked. In a panic, I scrambled around the outside of the building, trying every door and window as I went. They were all locked and there wasn't a sign of anyone inside who might let me in. Eventually, I realised that there was nothing for it but to ring the bell. Of course, it was Sr.

Agnes who answered. She told me I was no better than a prostitute and dragged me upstairs to the oratory, where she completely lost it. I'll never forget her face or my screams as, for a full hour, she battered me. Oh, it was horrible. After that, I thought, By Jaysus, you'll never do that to me again.

However, there would be one more round before Sr. Agnes was finally done with me. It was at the beginning of Leaving Cert year, when I was seventeen. That particular morning, she called us for mass and I decided I wasn't going to go. I had been working hard to get my grades back on track and I was stressed and exhausted but, beyond all of that, I was just sick of going to early mass. When Sr. Agnes came into my room, I told her, 'I'm not going. I'm too tired.' Her expression soured but she said nothing and walked out with the other girls. I took a moment to revel in my little victory, then turned over and went back to sleep. Three-quarters of an hour later, when she returned from mass, I was still in bed. I heard her before I saw her: the low ominous beat of her footsteps in the corridor. Then the door was thrown open and she stalked into my bedroom and hit me hard across the face. I turned away from her, holding my cheek, but she pulled me out of bed by my hair and shoved me onto the ground. I braced myself for her kicks but, with that, as suddenly as she had arrived, she left again.

Sitting on the cold floor, my face and scalp still

stinging, I was overcome with rage. It was as though the pent-up anger from all the years of beatings and name-calling and shaming rose up in me and I did something I had never done before: I ran after Sr. Agnes and, when I caught up with her in one of the dormitories, I hit her back. In fact, truth to tell, I had to be pulled off her. My retaliation signalled the last time that Sr. Agnes ever touched me. She was a bully but, when you stood up to her, she couldn't take it.

5

Leaving St. Joseph's

Sr. Agnes kept her distance from me for the remainder of my final year at St. Joseph's. In the absence of her constant bullying, I could focus on my studies in a way I had never been able to before. I wasn't a model student, by any means, but I enjoyed most of the subjects I was taking and the fact that I wasn't living every day in fear, or suffering regular beatings, meant that I could concentrate, retain information, do my homework in peace and show up for school on time.

Having failed my Inter, I knew that the Leaving Cert would be my last chance to leave the orphanage with a qualification or to have any hope of pursuing a professional career. I had a very particular career in mind. As a child, I had dreamed of becoming a nurse, but, in the past few years, a very different plan had emerged and it was all because of Sr. Agnes. From very early on in her tenure at St. Joseph's, I knew her behaviour to me was very wrong but I knew, too, that there was nothing I could do about it. In Ireland in the 1970s, if a child complained about the behaviour of a nun in an industrial school, it was the child who was punished. The testimony of a priest, nun, teacher or any other authority figure would have far outweighed that of a young girl, so I began to fantasise about becoming an authority figure myself and standing up for the rights of other children who were being bullied and beaten. Because it was justice that I lacked, I decided I wanted to join An Garda Síochána.

There were many aspects of the job I found appealing. I liked the idea of standing up to thieves and burglars and anyone who terrorised other people. I also imagined that, if I was a guard, I would finally be treated with respect: if I put my hand up, people would have to stop; if I told someone that what they were doing was wrong, they would have to listen. To me, though, being a guard meant more than merely enforcing the law; it meant having a caring role in society, helping people who were in trouble or distress and maybe even making a difference to their lives.

The fact that there were very few women in the guards never entered my head. I knew that there *were* women in the force, even if I had never seen one myself, and I knew I was capable of doing the work, so my thoughts revolved around what I would bring to the job and what a career like that could bring to my life. I never considered the difficulties I might experience as one of a small minority in the force.

In March 1980, three months before the Leaving Cert, we had a career guidance day in the school. A selection of representatives from various organisations, companies and professions came in to talk to us about our options. The only people I was interested in speaking to were the guards. Two of them, a sergeant and an officer, stood out in their peaked caps and uniforms. I recognised the sergeant, Sergeant Gordon, immediately. His daughter was two years ahead of me in St. Mary's and I had always been in awe of her because her father was a garda sergeant. I introduced myself to the pair of them and asked some basic questions about the job and what it entailed. They told me it was a great job, that the gardaí were pillars of the community and Sergeant Gordon added that the real joy of being a guard was the fact that you didn't just meet really bad people, you also met really good people. It was a pleasant, if unenlightening, conversation, and by the end of it I was determined to join the force.

For the next twelve weeks, I studied harder than I ever had before. There was no question now of sneaking out of the orphanage for a bag of chips or a rendezvous with Shane O'Connor – if I saw him at all, it was for a few minutes before or after confession and that was it. Nor was I engaging in any giddiness or other antics in class. My focus was on achieving something close to my potential in the limited time that was left to me before the Leaving Cert. I had a lot of ground to make up. Throughout my years in secondary school, the most consistent remark on my report cards was that I could be, and should be, doing much better than I was, but that I lacked application. Now, at last, I was applying myself but, with so little time left before the exams, would it be enough to rectify the shortcomings of the previous four years? In the end, I crammed the entire Leaving Cert syllabus into those last three months.

In the middle of the exams, on 10 June 1980, I turned eighteen. That meant that, as soon as the exams were over, I would be leaving St. Joseph's. I had mixed feelings about my departure. Although it would mean an end to the years of misery with Sr. Agnes, the fact remained that life in the orphanage was the only life I had ever known. There was security and stability there and something like the structure of a family. These were the people I had been reared with, the people who knew my inner thoughts, and soon they would be gone and, after more than sixteen years, I would once again be starting a new life on my own.

I knew that everyone had to leave the orphanage

eventually. Three of my sisters had left in 1973, and the fourth, Teresa, in 1978. Marguerite, who was the eldest of 'Sister Claire's girls', had departed the previous year, in 1979, to go and live with her father. Only Betty, Marie and I were left to say goodbye to each other. Still, if I was given the choice, I would have remained in the orphanage forever instead of leaving for Dublin and my family. At eighteen years old, I was off to live in a big city, with people I didn't know, with no job prospects and not a penny to my name. It's no wonder I was feeling ambivalent.

But before that I had to make my debut into Mallow society, when the Saint Mary's Secondary School debs ball took place on 5 July. Several weeks earlier, I had asked my day pupil friend, Ciara, to see if Shane would be my date and he had agreed. We had already made our own debs dresses in home economics class. The dresses had to be white, as a rule, and the material we had been given was a particularly unlovely polyester. Still, I thought I had done quite a good job with my own dress, under the circumstances, and, when Betty and Marie and I were rigged out in our handmade finery, we looked very well indeed.

At seven o'clock, Shane and the other boys came up to St. Joseph's to collect us. We had our photo taken in the parlour by Sr. Agnes and I took great satisfaction in introducing her to my date for the evening. 'Look at the man I have, Sr. Agnes', I wanted to say to her, 'and isn't he a fine thing?' Instead, for Shane's sake, I was polite and demure until the six of us went off together. As we walked to the Central Hotel, a sense of freedom overtook me and I felt so giddy that I skipped down the footpath. We were out on the streets of Mallow, with boys, and for once, I wasn't looking over my shoulder and I didn't care who saw us. That night, for the first time, it felt as though Betty and Marie and I could do whatever we wanted. We weren't 'the girls from the orphanage' anymore; we were just like everybody else. We belonged to the real world.

The evening began with a sit-down dinner. I recognised some of the Mercy sisters who taught in St. Mary's at the various tables but I didn't acknowledge them. I had no intention of being disrespectful to anyone but the days of bowing and scraping to nuns were finally at an end. I had finished my exams, I was leaving St. Joseph's and they had no power over me anymore. I ordered a pint of Harp to the table and, if any of them disapproved, they didn't say a thing about it.

After the dancing, a gang of us headed up the town, day girls and St. Joseph's girls and our partners, all together. We bought chips and stood around chatting for a bit, then we all dispersed and went our separate ways. Shane walked me back to the orphanage and gave me a proper kiss at the gate – no pecks on the cheek this time. Then I walked up the drive and in the front door, a St. Joseph's girl no more, a real woman at last.

The following day, I packed my meagre belongings into a suitcase and set off for Dublin.

6

The big smoke

The house on Shandon Road was an Edwardian redbrick, built in the early years of the twentieth century. My father had worked as a painter and decorator in England and the house was nicely appointed, with cast iron fireplaces in the bedrooms, a gilt mirror in the sitting room and a stained-glass window at the top of the stairs. To me, though, despite its high ceilings, the house was a confining space. It felt so much smaller than St. Joseph's: I was used to roaming around three storeys of big rooms and wide corridors and this was just an ordinary, three-bedroom house.

For any young adult, moving from an orphanage into a house would be a big change, but moving from the orphanage into a *family home* felt even stranger. It seemed surreal, at eighteen years of age, to be living in a house with my father, stepmother and sisters, when I hadn't been allowed to live like that as a child. Here we all were, together at last, living like a normal family, but to me it felt anything but normal. In reality, I was a total stranger to them, just as they were to me.

When my father was at home, the house felt claustrophobic. Having grown up around women, this strange, lumbering, masculine presence made me feel ill at ease. He was a big, powerful man and very reserved, and neither trait was softened by any sign of affection. Though he was very good to my stepmother, Kitty, his love was not something that was available to me. I cannot remember a single occasion where the two of us sat companionably together and had a proper conversation. When he came into a room, my whole body would stiffen.

When he was out of the house or away working, the atmosphere changed completely. Kitty and I would chat away to each other about anything and everything. Kitty was kind and, even though she had made it very clear that I was never to call her 'Mammy', there was something maternal about her – she would always have breakfast on the table for me in the morning and a hot water bottle waiting for me in the bed at night. She was great at cooking big country dinners and baking bread and scones or apple cake. She had three sisters, whom we called Auntie Ann, Auntie Rita and Auntie Hannah and, when they came to visit, Kitty would come alive. She would make a big meal of bacon and cabbage or lamb chops and we would all sit down together and they would talk and laugh about Cork and the people they knew when they were growing up. They took a real interest in my sisters and me and always asked how we were getting on. I loved spending time with them and those evenings with the Heskin sisters were some of the nicest I ever spent in Shandon Road. Eventually, though, my father would come home and, as soon as he stepped over the threshold, my fear and discomfort would return.

The fact was that I resented my father. Our relationship had always been strained, and living under the same roof had done nothing to improve it. If anything, it had made things worse. I constantly wondered why, now that I was grown and finished my schooling, I was living with the man who had sent me away when I needed him most. Who was this man to call himself my father when he had never fulfilled the role of a parent? Who was he to demand obedience and respect from the children he had abandoned? After nearly seventeen years in an orphanage, I had no interest in exchanging one set of rules – and one overbearing authority figure – for another. If I wanted to leave my bedroom looking like a bombsite, then that's what I was going to do; if I wanted to go out, then, by God, I was going out!

My sisters Catherine and Teresa were still living in Shandon Road when I came to Dublin. Catherine, the eldest, had a room to herself at the front of the house and I shared a bedroom with Teresa, who was just a few years older than me. Both Catherine and Teresa were very good to me in different ways and it was through the two of them that I started to familiarise myself with the big, strange city that was now home. Catherine was very generous. She bought clothes for me and took me to the cinema and the theatre and to concerts such as Johnny Cash at the State Cinema in Phibsborough. Teresa had been working as a telephonist at the Department of Posts and Telegraphs in Exchequer Street for the past three years and she already knew Dublin very well. She and I both loved traditional music and ballads, so we started to spend occasional evenings in the various pubs around town, where you could find ballad sessions every night of the week. We walked everywhere – we never took buses or taxis – so, in no time at all, I got to know the streets around Phibsborough and the inner city.

Teresa and I had lived separate lives while we were in St. Joseph's, and I was only truly getting to know my sister's personality now. She was great fun. We shared a bedroom and a social life, and we could hardly keep a straight face when we were together. In the evenings, when the news was on the television, no one was allowed to say anything that might distract my father. We all sat around in nervous silence, until Teresa looked at me or I looked at her, and the two of us would burst out laughing. We were always sent out of the room at once.

One night in August, when I had been living in Shandon Road for about a month, Teresa and I went out together to the International Bar in Wicklow Street. It was a warm summer evening and there was a ballad session on, so we were feeling particularly delighted with ourselves. Teresa was meeting her boyfriend, a Dubliner by the name of Joe Fox, and since I was still seeing Shane O'Connor from Mallow, I was going along to be the third wheel! It was a wonderful night. On the walk home, Teresa and I serenaded strangers with our own version of the folk song 'Mary Mack':

> *Johnny Mack's father's making Johnny Mack marry me,*
> *My father's making me marry Johnny Mack.*
> *I'm going to marry Johnny so my Johnny will take care of me,*
> *We'll all be feeling merry when I marry Johnny Mack.*

When we got back to Shandon Road, it was about two o'clock in the morning and the house was in complete darkness. Teresa and I glanced at each other, relieved. But the moment Teresa put her key in the front door, a light went on in the kitchen. My father was up and waiting for us. He met us in the hallway as we came in, shouting, 'How dare you come in at this hour of the morning!' We stood there in terror, occasionally stammering monosyllabic answers, as he ranted and roared at us both and told us that we could leave his house at once. Eventually, he sent us to our room. As we undressed in the dark, I could still feel the blood pulsing in my ears and I barely heard Teresa the first time she hissed, 'Let's go.'

'What?' I whispered.

'Let's go,' she said again. 'He doesn't want us here and I don't want to stay another minute. Let's leave in the morning.'

And leave we did. As soon as our father went off to work, we packed our belongings into two black bags and walked out the front door. Full of righteous indignation, we had almost reached O'Connell Street before it occurred to me that I hadn't the slightest idea how to find somewhere to live. Fortunately, Teresa had seen enough people arrive at the Department of Posts and Telegraphs from the country to know that the classifieds section of the *Irish Press* was the place to look. She sent me into a café to order us some breakfast while she got the newspaper and we spent the next hour poring over the advertisements as we ate our tea and toast. I spotted a place to let in Grosvenor Square in Rathmines, which sounded like a very glamorous address, so we called the landlord and arranged a viewing for that very day.

The flat in Grosvenor Square was really just a bedsit in the basement of a big Victorian house, with two beds in it, and a communal bathroom. The kitchen area consisted of a freestanding cooker with a two-ring hob, a small fridge and a sink. Rent was £25 a week, which Teresa thought was reasonable and I thought was a fortune, but the landlord was a guard, which I regarded as auspicious, so we decided to take it. Since we had brought all of our earthly belongings with us in the black bags, there was nothing to stop us moving in right away. That night, we feasted on beans on toast in our little room, scarcely believing how far our bravado had taken us.

The following morning, we cleaned the flat from top to bottom, then headed out to meet Joe and look for a job for me, so that I could pay my half of the rent. The three of us made our way down the Rathmines Road and over the La Touche Bridge to South Richmond Street, calling into every business we passed to see if they had any vacancies. On Wexford Street, I spotted a sign on the door of a café saying 'Waitress Wanted'. Moments after enquiring at the counter, I was ushered into the back room for an interview and about five minutes later I was told I could start the following day.

Café Angelo was owned by two brothers, John and

Paul Andreucetti. Despite the Andreucettis' Italian heritage, which had pride of place on the menus, the café was Dublin to the core. The Andreucetti family had been serving food in the area since 1913 and the clientele in Café Angelo represented a cross-section of Dublin society. The sit-down restaurant was full of couples and single people in their sixties and seventies who had the same plate of fish and chips with a slice of bread every evening for their tea, while the take-away was popular with office workers from nearby Harcourt Street, who would come in for a bag of chips on their way home from work.

My job was to clear the tables and take the orders. I had never waitressed before in my life and, what's more, I couldn't understand the Dublin accent, so the first few days were challenging. I can still remember trying to figure out what it meant when a customer asked for 'a one and one, love, and peas' or 'a fish supper and a cup of tea'. But working in that café really opened my eyes to the goodness of people. The Andreucettis were kind and easy to work for and the patrons, who clearly didn't have much money themselves, were always certain to leave a tip. That's not to say I wasn't occasionally tempted to pour a cup of tea over someone who was being rude or rowdy! But I never did, because I needed that job.

Café Angelo closed at six o'clock every day, so Teresa and I had our evenings to ourselves. Most days

we went to the Lower Deck pub in Portobello to listen
to music and, after that, we took turns to cook the
dinner. On a Saturday, when we knew our father would
be out, we sometimes went over to Shandon Road to
spend time with Kitty and her sisters. They always
greeted us warmly and never said anything about the
circumstances of our departure from the house. Auntie
Ann would tease me about working in a chipper and
say that she hoped I'd knuckle down and choose a real
career once I got my Leaving Cert results. Ann was
convinced I had done a great Leaving, though I wasn't
so sure myself.

The odd weekend, Shane would come up from
Mallow to visit me. We'd go on double dates with Teresa
and Joe and have a ball together at ballad sessions or
the pictures. Shane got on well with everybody and
my sister and her boyfriend were mad about him. I
loved spending time in his company. When I was with
him, he made me feel very special, holding my hand or
putting his arm around me, and he was always game
for a laugh. One weekend, I dared him to go and get
his ear pierced – it was 1980, after all, and that's what
all the men were doing! – so he went off and got it
done, just like that. We laughed about it all weekend
– I don't think I ever stopped laughing when he was
around.

I lost my virginity to Shane in that little flat in
Grosvenor Square. It was lovely and intimate, just as I

had expected my first time would be. I knew nothing at all about sex but Shane was careful and thoughtful and so kind. Of course, it helped that he looked like a film star! In all of the sadnesses that followed in my life, I often looked back and thought that, at least I had nothing to regret about my first sexual experience.

Sometimes I'd go back to Mallow to see Shane and we'd visit his sister, Mary, or go for a drink in the Hibernian Hotel. Whenever I was in town, I always made a point of dropping into St. Joseph's with some sweets for the little girls. Sr. Agnes would often be the one to answer the door and always behaved with the utmost civility, inviting me in and offering me a cup of tea or an apple. I could never accept anything from her, knowing that she would never have given me anything of the sort when I was a child in her care. On one occasion, I said as much to her. 'You were always an unpleasant girl,' she retorted with a snarl but I didn't care what she thought of me now. Instead of enduring her hospitality, I would go and have a cup of tea in the convent with Sr. Claire, who always treated me like a queen, bringing out the good china cups and the best cakes.

Throughout that summer, the Leaving Cert results were never far from my mind. I never discussed them with anyone, not even when I was teased about them by Auntie Ann. I didn't want to let on that I cared or that I was thinking about them at all. Failing the Inter

Cert had been the great humiliation of my life up to that point, and the names that Sr. Agnes had called me afterwards were still a source of mortification. I felt that I had done enough to pass the Leaving Cert but I was plagued with doubt and uncertainty.

On the morning of 12 August, I woke with a start. Teresa had thrown herself onto the end of my bed and was smiling at me expectantly. 'Well?' she asked, 'When are you going to get your results? I have to leave at 8.30 at the latest. Do you think the school will give them out to you before then?' I pulled the blankets over my head. 'I'm not calling the school,' I said. 'Who cares what I got in the Leaving? Sure don't I have a job already?'

Teresa was disappointed. She had been looking forward to a bit of diversion. 'Why did you take the day off work if you weren't going to get your results?' she asked grumpily. 'So I could get a bit of sleep,' I lied. 'But of course you've ruined any chance of that.' I sulked under the blankets while Teresa got ready for work. As she was walking out the door, she called back, a little ominously, I thought, 'You'll have to find out sooner or later.' And with that, she was gone.

There was no hope of getting back to sleep. Nevertheless, I stayed in bed and tried to avoid thinking of what was currently sitting in the secretary's office in St. Mary's Secondary School. This proved to be impossible. Eventually, I got dressed and paced around the flat until noon, when the anxiety became too much and I ran out to a payphone to ring Shandon Road. I hoped someone in the house would have called the school on my behalf and could put me out of my misery. The squeal on the other end of the line was so loud that I could barely make out a word. Auntie Ann, it seemed, had called St. Mary's and was delighted to learn that I had passed the Leaving Cert and so impatient to impart the news to me that her voice had been reduced to a sort of high-pitched scream.

I was elated and relieved and felt like running all the way to Shandon Road. I thought about the shame I had carried ever since I failed the Inter Cert and of the many times Sr. Agnes had called me an idiot and a dunce and all I could do was laugh. I had passed with honours. I could be anything I wanted now.

7

The world of work

Although it wasn't what you would describe as serious, my relationship with Shane O'Connor was a great source of happiness to me during those first months in Dublin. His letters, full of the latest gossip from Mallow, and his occasional visits, brought lightness and levity to an otherwise stressful time. Teresa and I were struggling to support ourselves and pay the rent – there was one week when the only way we managed to eat at all was because Teresa had found a pound on the footpath on Camden Street!

One Sunday in October, Shane and I were in Heuston Station at the end of another visit. He had been more subdued than usual that weekend and, as we waited for the Cork train to pull into the platform, he became agitated, as though there was something he wanted to say. When I asked him what was the matter, he seemed almost relieved, as though a moment he had been dreading had finally arrived.

'This isn't going to work,' he said. 'My life is in Mallow and yours is in Dublin and we can't keep pretending that a weekend here and there makes for a real relationship.' I shouldn't have been surprised – his trips to Dublin had become more and more infrequent – but I was. And I was devastated. 'You're probably right,' I said, struggling to contain my emotions. 'It's a long distance for you to travel just to see me.'

'Ah, Jel,' he said, his voice still full of kindness, 'that's not it at all. It's just that it feels like we have to get on with things. Start planning a real future. And I can't do that if I'm spending all of my time jumping on trains and writing letters.'

'I completely understand,' I said, trying to sound dignified. 'You have to do what's best for you and I don't want to be a distraction.' I said nothing at all after that, but dug my nails into my hands to retain my composure as he kissed me on the cheek and boarded the train. I walked out of the station with no sense at all of where I was going and stopped on the Seán Heuston Bridge and just cried for a quarter of an hour. Every negative thought I had ever had about myself returned, unbidden, into my head and I found myself thinking, 'How could you, Majella Moynihan, a St.

Joseph's girl, ever have thought that you would be good enough for handsome, *lovely* Shane O'Connor?' I don't know how I made it home to Rathmines that night but I know that I cried myself to sleep.

A few weeks later, I was back down in Mallow and on my way to visit Sr. Claire in the convent when I bumped into Ciara Willis, my old school friend. Ciara and Shane had always been very friendly so, after warm hellos and a quick summary of all our recent exploits, I asked her a little awkwardly if she had seen anything of him in the last while. She confessed that she had and then paused, looking anywhere but at me. 'Go on,' I said. 'Just tell me and get it over with.' Ciara told me that Shane had a new girlfriend from the town. Although they hadn't been together for very long, I realised at once that it was this girl – or, more accurately, Shane's feelings for her – that had been the real reason for our break-up. I was heartbroken. I took my leave of Ciara in a daze and hardly absorbed a single word that Sr. Claire said to me over tea and scones.

Later, on the bus, I felt that my years in Mallow and St. Joseph's were definitely behind me. Shane's visits to me and mine to him had kept me connected to that time in my life and, now, all that was at an end.

I decided that it was time to leave Café Angelo and seek out a more suitable position for myself. I didn't feel ready to apply for the guards just yet – I wanted more experience in the world first – so instead I went for a job as a catering assistant in St. Vincent's Private Hospital. Although there wasn't a huge difference between the work of a waitress and that of a catering assistant, it felt more meaningful to be helping sick people in a hospital and, besides, the pay was double what I was getting in the chipper, so it would put an end to my money woes. I was delighted when I got the position.

Built in the early 1970s, and opened in 1974, St. Vincent's Private shared a site with the larger St. Vincent's Hospital at Elm Park on the Merrion Road. The hospital was owned by the Sisters of Charity, and at the official opening, Archbishop John Charles McQuaid had noted: 'It is the unchanging character of a Catholic hospital that every member of its staff accepts with clear assent and fulfils with scrupulous exactitude the moral law that regulates their therapy.'

To what extent he meant his edict to apply to the catering staff, only the archbishop himself could have told you. Staff in that department were, for the most part, young, exuberant and very sociable. We worked two different shifts, which alternated week to week: the morning shift from 7 a.m. to 3 p.m. and the evening shift from 1 p.m. to 9 p.m. The job of the assistants was to take meal orders from patients, prepare the trays and hand them out, collect the trays when the patients had eaten and wash the dishes. We also gave out tea and coffee to visitors but these were strictly rationed – I had to tell more than one celebrity patient, including a sitting taoiseach, that they were allowed one tea or coffee for one visitor only! Still, the patients and staff got on very nicely together and the catering assistants used to do very well with tips.

The woman in charge of the catering staff was a nun called Sr. Rosario. She was a real dictator, always finding fault with everything we did but she had great time for me. She would arrive in my kitchenette and exclaim, 'Oh, Majella, your kitchen is spotless, it's a credit to you,' and I would say, 'I know, Sister. Thank you very much.' After a few weeks, she offered me accommodation on campus. I gratefully accepted, glad that I wouldn't have to get up at 5 a.m. anymore to make the morning shift, though I was sad to leave Teresa and the flat in Grosvenor Square. Despite our occasional financial hardships, we had had a happy time there together.

The accommodation for the female catering staff in St. Vincent's was in a building called St. Rita's, a large, grey cement block with four storeys and over one hundred rooms. We each had our own room, with a bed and a little sink and access to the communal bathrooms, of which there were two on every floor. Meals and electricity were provided at a very reasonable price, with the cost taken out of our wages. The door was locked at midnight and, if you came home any later, you would have to ask a security guard to unlock it for you. It was an institution, just like the institution in which I had grown up and, though I didn't like to admit it, I felt perfectly at home in that environment. The work was easy and I enjoyed it, and the other girls were brilliant fun.

We started going to dances, first at the National Ballroom and the Ierne Hall, both of which were on Parnell Square. Every Friday and Saturday night we'd get all dolled up in our jumpsuits, culottes and cheesecloth and get the bus over to the northside. Although it was the 80s, the music in both venues was played by showbands and the dominant dance styles were still jiving and waltzing. There were never any slow sets – intimacy and proximity were not to be encouraged, even in a dance hall! The venues were full of young people, many of them from the country, and the atmosphere at the start of a night was not unlike a cattle mart, with the girls lined up on one side of the room and the boys on the other. The boys would look at the girls across the dance floor, then start to make their way over. If you saw one of them coming and you didn't like the look of him, you would pretend to be engrossed in conversation with your friends! If you liked someone, you would go out on the floor with him for a few dances and then, at the end of the night, you would thank him and leave him at the door. It was very seldom that one of our gang went off with anyone after a dance.

In this way, the months passed by. I worked hard in the hospital – Sr. Rosario had already begun to hint that I could expect to make supervisory rank one day – and I enjoyed my social life with the girls. Those were some of the happiest times of my life: my work was fulfilling and enabled me to show the caring side of my personality and the rest of my life was carefree. I wasn't answerable to anybody. I could do what I liked and I always had money. If I wanted to go to the cinema, I went to the cinema; if I wanted to go to the theatre, I went to the theatre, and I always attended mass. I went to the Canaries and, later, to Portugal with the girls from St. Vincent's and we lived it up. I had no interest in having a boyfriend – the girls were all single and when we went out, we went out together in groups. We would go to the Lower Deck and listen to music or go to a dancehall and dance with whoever asked us and have a few drinks. Afterwards, we would all head back to St. Rita's and stay up late in each other's rooms, rehashing the events of the night.

In the summer of 1981, I got a letter from Ciara Willis letting me know that Shane was engaged to be married. I had to read the letter three times before I could absorb the information. I couldn't believe he had proposed to his new girlfriend so quickly and such a short time after he and I had broken up. Still, after the initial shock and displeasure had subsided, I was able to wish them both well. Whenever I thought of him afterwards, I remembered only his sweetness.

8

A chance encounter

When it came to our social life, the girls of St. Vincent's were always on the lookout for novelty, so when Edel Quinn, who was the youngest of the catering assistants and my best friend, heard there were dances on in the Garda Club, it caused a flurry of excitement. For myself, especially, the prospect of being in a room full of guards, of seeing how they behaved in their spare time and talking to them about the job, was nothing less than exhilarating. I was anxious to go and arranged that we would all attend the very next dance at the club on Harrington Street, the following Thursday night.

The Garda Club had two ballrooms, as well as a members' bar in the basement, all of which were usually packed on Mondays and Thursdays, when the dances were held. In the 1970s and 80s, many unmarried members of the force in Dublin lived in accommodation attached to garda stations such as Harcourt Terrace and Pearse Street, and socialised in the club, which was also open to members of the public. Two guards stood at the door and served as bouncers when there was a dance on, looking everyone up and down, appraising their clothes and shoes and their behaviour. The girls and I fixed each other's hair and checked our lipstick, determined that nothing should thwart our plans for the evening. As we sailed past the bouncers and into the venue, I was full of anticipation.

Reality was always going to fall short of my expectations. A dance in the Garda Club turned out to be much like a dance anywhere else. Groups of guards stood around in 'half blue' – wearing the trousers and shirts from their uniforms but without the tunic or cap – throwing back pints of lager and stout and checking out the girls on the dance floor. Far from the gods of my imagination, most of them were just young lads up from the country, enjoying their first experiences of the Dublin social scene. They seemed content in their own company and not the least bit approachable, so I dismissed any thoughts of chatting to them about their work and joined my friends. Still, the music was good and there was a nice crowd, so I was perfectly satisfied with the evening.

We hadn't been in the club very long when a man

with red hair and blue eyes came over and asked me to dance. Looking back now, I don't recall any great sense of enthusiasm when he approached me and proffered his hand. But I had been longing to get out onto the dance floor, so off I went. When the song ended, he told me his name was Fintan. I thanked him and went back to my friends. Later, when the girls and I were jiving and laughing together, Fintan came back to ask for another dance. Afterwards, I introduced him to Edel, Lucy, Florence and Catherine and we all had a drink together. He told me he was from Cavan but living in Rathmines and working as a barman in town. At the end of the night, he asked if I'd come and meet him sometime in the city centre bar where he worked. I agreed, so we made a date and then I jumped into a taxi with the girls.

The list of pubs I frequented during my first year in Dublin was a short one: the Merrion Inn, which was on Merrion Road, across from the hospital campus, was where the girls and I used to go in the evenings after work or for a drink or two on a Friday or Saturday night before we got the bus into town to go to a dance. Other than that, there was the Lower Deck and the International Bar, where I went to ballad sessions, and that was it. I had never been to the bar where Fintan worked, an attractive relic from the Victorian era, with mahogany panelling and stained-glass windows. The first night I went there to meet him, I brought a gang of girls from the hospital.

That night, I sat perched on a stool at the main bar, while Fintan chatted to me and the girls, when he wasn't pouring pints or joking with regulars. He seemed pleased for me to see him in work mode, proud of his rapport with the patrons and his unconventional sense of humour.

It was June and the weather was fine, so the pub was thronged with tourists and revellers. I stayed at the bar talking to Fintan until closing time, then waited as he and the rest of the staff closed up. He gave us a round of free drinks, which really impressed the girls, then escorted us all to the taxi rank. As we made our way to St. Stephen's Green, he and I lagged behind the group a little, chatting. I asked if he often went to the Garda Club, and that was when he told me he had applied for Templemore. I could barely hide my surprise. 'Really?' I exclaimed. 'I didn't know they were hiring.' 'They were,' said Fintan. 'I don't know if they still are. I applied weeks ago.'

A prospective guard. I felt a potent mix of fascination and envy. What had previously been an unremarkable date had suddenly become very interesting indeed. Joining the guards was still my dearest aspiration and anyone else who shared my dream was, I thought, a kindred spirit. It was a big point in Fintan's favour and it allayed any lurking doubts about our compatibility.

I kissed him goodnight and we arranged to meet again soon.

Over the following months, Fintan and I saw each other twice or three times a week, sometimes in the pub where he worked, sometimes in the Garda Club or the Lower Deck and sometimes we just went to the pictures. After we had been going out for a few months, we started sleeping together in Fintan's digs in Rathmines. I was always terrified of getting caught by the landlord. I usually stayed over on a Friday or Saturday night and, the morning after, Fintan would have to get up and go to work for 10 a.m. I was usually off at weekends, so I'd stay in his room and sleep on after he left. Once I was up and ready to go myself, I'd wait until the house was completely silent before sneaking downstairs. I couldn't bear the thought of meeting Fintan's landlord on my way out.

Fintan used condoms that he got in the North as, back then, contraception in the Republic was only available on prescription. By 1982, the campaign for the government to introduce a pro-life amendment to the constitution was in full swing and it was a strange time to be in a sexual relationship, especially if you weren't married. Although I suspected then and know now, as a result of conversations we had over the years, that my friends were having sex, it was a topic we never broached with each other at the time. We were all afraid. Afraid of going further and doing more than our friends were doing. Afraid of being regarded as wild or a 'slut'. I knew about the Irish Family Planning clinic, and that it was a place where women could get advice about contraception, and I knew that Irish women sometimes went to England to have abortions but, as far as I was aware, no one I knew had availed of either service.

Although Fintan was always generous to me and my friends whenever we went out together and always very complimentary to me, I never really felt settled or happy in the relationship. By October 1982, I had decided to end things. I told him I wanted us to break up, that I didn't love him. He was upset and asked me to reconsider, but I was resolved. As I was leaving, he told me that he had just found out that he had been accepted into the guards and was going to Templemore in December.

An Garda Síochána only held recruitment drives once or twice a year. These were advertised in the paper and generally attracted thousands of applicants. Since the guards did not accept applications outside of these recruitment campaigns and I had missed the hiring round to which Fintan had applied, I had assumed that I would have to wait another twelve months before I could try my luck.

One Tuesday morning, in St. Rita's, I was awakened by a yell: 'Majella Moynihan! Phone call!' I put on my slippers and ran down to the big booth in the lobby.

It was Auntie Ann calling from her house in Youghal. 'Well,' she said, 'did you buy the *Irish Press* yet today? Because there's something in it that might interest you.' When I asked what it was, she replied, 'All I'll say is this: I still think the nursing would suit you better,' and then she hung up. It was all very cryptic. I hurried down to the hospital shop to get the paper. I was dying to know what was inside but waited until I was back in the privacy of my room to find out. I rifled through the pages until, eventually, among the classifieds, I found an advertisement for An Garda Síochána, seeking to recruit men and women to the force. I put the paper down and felt a rush of excitement course through me. I hadn't missed my chance after all.

The advertisement directed all prospective applicants to apply at their local garda station. I went into Mountjoy station feeling as if I was about to complete a truly momentous task. In the event, though, all that happened was a young sergeant ushered me into a back room, told me a little bit about the role of the gardaí in the community and gave me a form to fill out. I was required to submit my own basic information, as well as a list of all my relatives and their addresses, so that they could be vetted by the guards to ensure that I was a suitable candidate. I was then asked to attend a medical examination at garda headquarters in the Phoenix Park.

The medical exam was very straightforward. At

the time, a female officer was required to be taller than five foot five inches, though this requirement has since been abolished and replaced with a physical competence test. Fortunately for me, I didn't have to run around and weave through cones or walk along a balance beam or be timed doing sit-ups and press-ups. I just had to be the height I was, five foot seven inches, and have my eyes, ears and breathing checked by the garda surgeon.

At last, I was called to interview. I was given one month to prepare and would then have to present myself at the Civil Service Commission in O'Connell Street. I was a nervous wreck for the whole month. As far as I was concerned, this would be the most important conversation of my life and I wasn't sure how to prime myself. I spent those four weekends in Phibsborough library, looking up everything I could think of about An Garda Síochána and, when I wasn't in the library I was observing guards on the beat. I wasn't quite satisfied with what I learned from either the reading or the observation but I reasoned there wasn't much more I could do.

I can still remember what I wore to the interview. It was a navy wool skirt suit by Michael Gall, the most expensive outfit I had ever owned. I wore it with navy leather gloves and a navy handbag and I felt like a million dollars. I had always spent as much as I could possibly afford on my clothes but I really pushed the boat out when I bought that suit. This was, after all, the ensemble that was going to change my life!

I was so nervous walking into the interview that I dropped my gloves. As I gathered myself, the senior guard who was to interview me introduced himself as Superintendent Con Cronin. He was flanked on both sides by two female civil servants. I had only just sat down when the superintendent smiled broadly and said, 'Tell me, Majella, who is the patron saint of Cullen?'

This may seem like a most unusual question in an interview for An Garda Síochána. But my interview took place in 1982 and, at that time, the Irish state and the Catholic Church were in such complete accord that no one in the room betrayed any hint of surprise. Besides, as an opening salvo, it served a dual purpose: it was a reminder that, in order to be a good bangharda, it was expected that I would be a good, clean-living Catholic and it also told me that Con Cronin had been looking into my background. Cullen, County Cork was just a few short miles from Knocknagree, where my mother was born, and Cullen itself was where she was buried.

I told him the patron saint of Cullen was Latheran, a holy woman who was known to have the ability to carry hot coals in her apron without getting burned. The story goes that, one day, Latheran went to the forge to gather some materials to light her fire. As she left, the blacksmith admired her bare feet and legs. Latheran was flattered and, looking down at her feet, she committed the sin of pride. Because of her sin, the coals, to which she had previously been impervious, caused her apron to catch fire and her legs and feet were burned. Such were the repercussions in Catholic Ireland for a woman taking pleasure in her own body!

The rest of the questions were more practical. Common sense in a recruit was prized above all things and it was Con Cronin's job to confirm that I had a brain. I was asked to imagine myself in various situations – a fire, a robbery – and consider how I would respond, as a guard. I referred as much as possible to the research that I had done over the previous weeks and cited the core objectives of policing, such as the preservation of peace and public order, the protection of life and property, the vindication of the human rights of each individual and the protection of the security of the state. I was able to answer the questions that were put to me and the superintendent seemed to approve. By the end, I felt that I had done well and performed to the best of my ability. As I left the room, I thought to myself, If I get it, I get it, and if I don't, I don't. And that was that.

Two weeks later, I got a call from Kitty to say that there was a letter for me in Shandon Road. 'Would you like me to open it for you?' she asked.

'No!' I cried. 'I'll open it myself. I'll be there within the hour.'

On tearing it open I saw that I'd been offered a place on the upcoming April 'D' training course at the garda college in Templemore. I was in – and I was over the moon!

9

Girl in blue

On 27 April 1983, I left Dublin for Templemore.

My sister Catherine was travelling to Templemore with me, to see me off. She beamed with pride as we queued for our tickets. When I finally reached the counter and asked for a single ticket to Templemore, she squeezed my arm and said, 'Let's get two tickets and I'll come with you!' Making the journey with me was a lovely gesture and I was delighted to have someone with whom I could share my excitement.

To say that I was happy would be putting it mildly. From the moment I received the letter telling me that I had been accepted to the garda training college, I had been in a near-constant state of elation. Few events in life can compare to achieving a childhood dream and

I hadn't been keeping quiet about it. I think I called almost everyone I knew to tell them that I had gotten into the guards. I had even written to Sr. Claire! Just about everyone I told was delighted for me – even my father had mustered a gruff 'Well done'.

The only place where the response was a little subdued was in St. Vincent's because this change in my circumstances meant that I would be leaving the hospital. My closest friends, Edel, Florence and Catherine, arranged a going-away party in the Merrion Inn and we cried the whole evening. Sr. Rosario seemed disappointed at first that I wasn't going to stay on and become a supervisor, but she rallied and, in the weeks when I was serving out my notice, she would respond to any reference to my joining the guards with a loud 'God love them.'

Shortly after the arrival of the acceptance letter, I received another item in the post: a Valentine's card from Fintan.

I hadn't heard from him since the break-up, so this was his first communication. I was taken aback to receive a Valentine's card, of all things, because, as far as I was concerned, we were finished. The return address was Templemore, County Tipperary. Of course, I knew he was at the college and that, for a short time at least, our courses would overlap, but this was a stark reminder that we would be seeing each other again and soon.

A few days after the Valentine's card arrived, I received another letter in the post: an invitation to Fintan's passing-out ceremony in Templemore that May. I decided, then, to give him a call. He seemed happy to hear from me, though a little apprehensive about what I was going to say. I thanked him for the card and the invitation and told him that, as it happened, I would be in Templemore myself in May. Fintan was stunned. 'You needn't think I'm chasing you,' I laughed. 'I've been accepted into the guards. You always knew I wanted to join.' I asked how he was getting on himself, and he said he was enjoying his time in the training college. He had no idea, as yet, where he was likely to be stationed but was hoping for Dublin or Cavan. It was a pleasant conversation, though not in the least romantic.

On the train down to Templemore, I chatted to Catherine, but every quiet moment was spent picturing myself as a qualified bangharda, imagining the kinds of conversations I would have while I was out on the beat and contemplating the ways in which I would be able to make the world a better place. My guiding principles were still those that I had formed as a lonely teenager in the orphanage, when all I wanted was for someone to tell me that I wasn't the brat I was being made out to be. Now I hoped I could be that person for other lonely teenagers. It was naive, I know, but completely sincere.

Catherine walked me to the gates of Templemore

and then she left to get the train back to Dublin. The sight of the college was overwhelming: a big stone army barracks with two large squares surrounded by looming grey buildings and lots of Portakabins.

All of the new recruits were asked to assemble in the hall. In total, there were about fifty-five of us including the April B, C and D intakes. I was delighted to see that there were other women there, eighteen recruit banghardaí – or 'banners', as we would soon be called – in total between the three classes. We were all asked to sign the following solemn declaration in the presence of a peace commissioner:

I hereby solemnly and sincerely declare before God that—

- I will faithfully discharge the duties of a member of the Garda Síochána with fairness, integrity, regard for human rights, diligence and impartiality, upholding the constitution and the laws and according equal respect to all people,
- While I continue to be a member, I will to the best of my skill and knowledge discharge all my duties according to law; and
- I do not belong to, and will not while I remain a member form, belong to or subscribe to, any political party or secret society whatsoever.

I was so nervous that I signed my name wrong. I was registered at Templemore under the name on my birth certificate, *Abina Majella Moynihan*, but twice I forgot to include Abina and had to ask for another copy of the declaration. I'm sure the registrars thought I was an awful fool. I wonder now whether it was an omen. I can only imagine how much happier my life would have been if, instead of signing that form, I had turned on my heels and run all the way back to Dublin and St. Vincent's Hospital.

Once we had signed, we were shown to our rooms. The banghardaí slept in a separate building and I was to share a room with two other women from my class. The bedroom was like an old dormitory. There were three single beds, a sink and a mirror and we each had a wardrobe and a shelf to store our belongings. It was very basic.

After that we went for tea in the mess along with the rest of the college. As I walked back from the counter with my tray, I saw Fintan at the other end of the room. He had spotted me too and gave a little nod. Then I joined the rest of my class. After the meal, on my way back to the dorms, Fintan caught up with me and asked how I was settling in. We chatted for a bit and he suggested we go for a drive that Saturday. I paused. I wasn't sure that I wanted to get back with Fintan but the college was big and daunting and it would be nice to know that at least one person cared how I was getting on. 'Sounds good,' I said. 'See you then.'

*

Life in Templemore was ordered and regimented. In the morning, we got up and cleaned the bedroom. Our rooms were checked twice a week to ensure that we had washed the floor and sink and dressed our beds appropriately. Once that was done, we had breakfast in the mess, after which we went out on parade, where our uniforms and general cleanliness were inspected. Then it was time for class. We studied Irish, first aid, physical education, swimming and shooting in the morning and in the afternoon we had police duties. Police duties was the most important subject on the syllabus at Templemore and it was also the most difficult. It was in this class that we learned about criminal law, professional competence, the roles and responsibilities of the guards and how to work with communities to maintain law and order. I found it fascinating.

Twice a week, we went out into the front square and had drill, where we all stood in lines and an instructor called out commands, then we all moved and marched in formation. Our drill sergeant claimed that this would familiarise us with the experience of operating as a unit but the real purpose was to prepare us for our passing-out ceremony on graduation day. In the evenings we studied until nine o'clock and then, several nights a week, we all went down to one of the pubs in Templemore, usually Polly's, which was just outside the gates of the college. Then back to our bedrooms by eleven and lights out shortly afterwards.

A few days after we arrived we were given our uniforms. I still remember how excited I was to wear mine for the first time. As soon as the tunic was on, I looked in the mirror, put my shoulders back and thought, *I've done it. I'm a guard.* The banners all had skirts – trousers didn't come in for banghardaí until the 90s – and the question of whether slacks should be included in the women's uniform was the subject of several discussions in the Dáil. The shoes were hideous; I hated them on sight, with their round toes, thin laces and Cuban heels. Only the men were given batons – senior gardaí were concerned that, if banghardaí had batons, criminals could easily take them and use them as a weapon. We were also given instructions as to how to wear our hair. Women with long hair had to pin it up. I had short hair and had to cut it shorter. Only an inch was permitted to be visible under the hat.

Uniforms had to be impeccable at all times and our shoes had to be shining. One day I was called out of parade to go over and see the superintendent because I had left a fingerprint on the peak of my hat.

'Why didn't you clean your hat?' he said.

'I did, Sir,' I replied. 'I did.'

'You did not,' he said. 'There was a mark on it.'

I had to report back to the office the following day with a pristine hat.

In all the time I had spent fantasising about myself as a garda, I had never devoted much energy to considering practicalities, such as the training and what would be involved. My focus had been on getting into Templemore and I assumed that once I was there, I would live happily ever after. It soon became apparent, however, that the schedule was rigorous and intensive and the classes were tough. Every one of us recruits had his or her shortcomings exposed and I know that we all felt, at times, as though we were floundering. In our first swimming class, I and another recruit, Stewart O'Sullivan, had to confess to the instructor that we couldn't swim. 'Go across the pool, then, like dogs,' he told us, 'and do the doggy paddle,' while the others swam lengths.

The academic classes were difficult too and, though I passed every test, I often did so by the skin of my teeth. My evenings were spent trying to keep up with my studies. Having spent weeks boasting about my great good fortune in being accepted into the guards, I couldn't fall at the final hurdle.

I still remember the police duties class when I was asked by Sergeant Dan Corrigan, 'Who can never be handcuffed?' The desired response was 'Women, children, the elderly and soldiers in uniform, Sir,' but to me, it sounded like a riddle and the answer eluded me. Through the fog of my confusion and panic, I heard the girl beside me whisper 'Cows!' and, since I had nothing better to say, I piped up, 'Cows, Sir!'

The whole class dissolved into hysterical laughter. I thought I'd never live it down.

Other challenges presented themselves outside the classroom. In the evenings the other recruits would bond in the pub or in the dorms by regaling those around them with stories from their childhood. Although I would laugh and joke with everyone, I rarely said anything about my own background. I didn't want anyone to know that I had been raised in an orphanage or that I had been left there by my father. Those months in Templemore were about making a good first impression with your future colleagues and superiors and the circumstances of my upbringing made me feel ashamed and inferior. So I kept to small talk and smiled and nodded when the conversation turned personal.

It was a relief to spend time with Fintan. At least I didn't have to explain anything to him about my childhood because he already knew everything there was to know. Fintan was one of the few recruits who had a car with him in Templemore, so we would go for drives or on dates together two or three times a week. On our drive together that first weekend, he asked, 'Could we start up again?'

'Yeah, I'd like that,' I replied. I didn't want to be alone.

Although the senior guards had made it clear from

our arrival that relationships between recruits were frowned upon, the reality was that there was plenty of fraternising going on in the college. We would hang around in groups in the pub, drinking and chatting, but, on the walk home, we paired off into couples. It was common knowledge – and the subject of much gossip – that people used to have sex down by the handball alley or around the back of the gym but public displays of affection were unthinkable and amorous behaviour of any kind, including kissing, was done outside the college, on pain of expulsion.

The life of a recruit bangharda in Templemore differed from that of the male recruits in ways that extended far beyond our uniforms. Although by 1983 women had been permitted to join An Garda Síochána for twenty-four years, we were still a small minority within the force and a minority, too, in the training college. That's not to say that some attempts weren't being made to improve the situation – the April 'A' class, for example, consisted entirely of female recruits. The teaching staff were exclusively male, however, and some of them might have benefited from some sensitivity training themselves, when it came to their attitudes to women. I can still remember our drill sergeant calling out during one of our manoeuvres: 'Open up your legs. You know you can do it – didn't you have them open in the back of the car last night?'

Regardless of how these kinds of comments made us feel, we laughed along, not knowing what else to do.

In May, Fintan graduated from Templemore. I attended his passing out in the Michael Gall skirt suit that I had worn to my interview and I met his family for the first time. Fintan had a younger brother and two younger sisters, all of whom were very sweet. His father had passed away and his mother was a well-to-do Cavan lady. Fintan was to be stationed in County Donegal and she was disappointed that he would be so far from home. The family went off for a meal together after the ceremony and I met up with Fintan and the rest of his class that night in the Templemore Arms.

We arranged to stay in touch. Once or twice a week, I would slip out of the college and call Fintan from a payphone on the main street of Templemore and, whenever possible, we'd meet in Dublin at the weekend. Sometimes we met in Cavan, where Fintan would stay with his family and I would stay with my sister Anne, who was living in Kilnaleck.

In July, Fintan invited me to Donegal for the weekend so I could see where he was stationed. I still can't believe that I made the trek from Tipperary to Donegal to visit a boyfriend, let alone that I would do so several times over the course of that summer. It was a terribly long and miserable journey, beginning with the train to Dublin followed by a four-and-a-half-hour bus ride. He had a room in a house in the village where he was stationed, which was owned by a pleasant woman called Mrs Grayson. Upon hearing that Fintan was having a girlfriend to stay, Mrs Grayson saw to it that I had my own room, as would have been regarded as right and proper at that time. There were several other guards living in the house and, although we never spent any time together, they were aware that I was visiting Fintan.

Back in Templemore, the senior guards were also aware that I was seeing another recruit and visiting him at weekends. On more than one occasion, I was questioned by Superintendent T.J. O'Sullivan about the relationship and why I was leaving the college for overnight trips. Although it was never explicitly stated that relationships were forbidden or that trainee guards were not permitted to have pre-marital sex, it was clear that the authorities in Templemore disapproved of my behaviour. I paid little heed to their meddling and wrote it off as the stuffiness of middle-aged men. After all, what business was it of theirs what I did in my spare time?

At the end of August, I arranged for Fintan to come and stay in the house in Shandon Road. It was Saturday and I remember we spent the evening at the Hut, a bar on the Phibsborough Road which was popular with prison guards from Mountjoy. When we got back to Shandon Road, everyone was in bed. My father and stepmother had a room at the back of the house, so they wouldn't have been disturbed when I crept up the stairs to the room that Kitty had made up for Fintan or when I crept back down an hour later.

That was the night our baby was conceived.

10

A pregnant recruit

From the moment that Fintan and I had sex that night in August, I knew I was pregnant. I can't explain it, all I can say is that my body felt different in a strange and indefinable way. I lay awake that night in my own bed and worried.

To become pregnant at twenty-one was not part of my plan. The plan was that I would get married in my late twenties or early thirties and then start a family. Before that, I wanted to live my life, enjoy my work and appreciate the independence that I had achieved for myself. I hoped that I would eventually meet someone kind and supportive and that, together we would have a lovely home with two or three children. I would give those children all the love I'd never had myself as a child. I knew I had a lot of love in me and I felt I had an extra special bond with children.

I never foresaw my future with Fintan, and I felt that he wasn't ready to be a father. If I was pregnant, would he walk away?

These were dark thoughts and not at all conducive to heading back to Templemore and getting on with my training, so the following morning I decided to put it out of my mind and carry on with my life. I had only three weeks to go until my final exams and plenty of study to do, so I got up early, Fintan and I went our separate ways, and I caught the train to Tipperary.

Back in Templemore my classes resumed. As we were in the latter stages of our training, I exerted myself more than ever. I ran, climbed, jumped, shot and attempted to swim. Once, during a game of soccer with some of the other banghardaí, I experienced a wave of nausea and had to run to the side of the pitch and vomit. I told the others it must have been something I had eaten at lunch but I knew there was another possible cause.

Those last few weeks were a flurry of activity. We were all frantically studying for our final exams and preparing for graduation. In drill class, we were learning the manoeuvres for our final parade and, back in the dorms, when we weren't revising our notes, we were walking through our steps. It was a tense time and the additional anxieties I was feeling made it all the more difficult to concentrate. As the days passed and my period failed to arrive it became harder to keep thoughts of pregnancy out of my head.

Shortly before our exams, one of the banghardaí from the all-female April 'A' class won the Rose of Tralee. Brenda Hyland had qualified for the pageant while she was in the training college, managing to get out of Templemore one weekend with a male friend who drove her to Waterford and back, without attracting any attention. When she was named Waterford Rose, Brenda could no longer avoid the notice of An Garda Síochána but, as it turned out, everyone in Templemore was delighted. As far as the guards were concerned, this meant an end to the image of the dull bangharda and Brenda, who was tall and attractive with dark hair and a wonderful smile, was the perfect ambassador for the force. She was given the use of the hall at lunchtime so she could prepare for her performance in Kerry and we often heard the strains of 'My Irish Mollie' sung in a lively voice. At the end of August, Brenda returned to the college with her sash and tiara and the recruits gave her a guard of honour and stood to attention, while she inspected us. Then we all trudged off to our rooms and went back to our studies.

We had final exams in swimming, shooting, first aid, PE, Irish and police duties. For the swimming exam, we had to climb up to a diving board and then dive into the deep end of the pool. I was terrified. I don't know how I got through it. I still remember splashing around in the water, convinced that I was going to drown, until, eventually, the instructor dangled a long pole into the pool. 'Hold on to that,' he called to me, and somehow I managed to do as he asked. After he had fished me out he said, 'Well, you're a non-swimmer anyway,' and that was that.

For the shooting exam, we had a shoot-off. I made it to the last two with another recruit but, in the end, he beat me by a point. We had all given a pound each into a pot, with the total to be given to the winner, £21 in all! I couldn't believe I had come so close to getting all that money, only to suffer such a narrow defeat!

First aid and PE were very straightforward but I'll never know how I passed Irish. In the oral exam I was asked how many banghardaí were in the garda band, and since I couldn't remember the word 'ceathrar', the Irish for 'four people', I just said, 'Four.' Not my finest hour.

Two days after the exams were over, three recruits from April 'D' class, myself included, were summoned to the office of Superintendent T.J. O'Sullivan. 'You have all,' he said, 'received a mark of 49 per cent in police duties. As you know well, a passing grade requires 50 per cent or over. All three of you have, therefore, failed.' I was devastated. Failed by a single per cent. I assumed that I wouldn't, now, be able to graduate with the rest of my class. Would I still be allowed to join the guards?

The superintendent paused for a moment before declaring that all three of us would be held back for an additional eight weeks, so that we could pass police duties. I was relieved that my career hadn't ended before it had begun, though I was disappointed to have to stay on in the college and miss passing out with my friends. In the end, though, I need not have worried. When the final results went up on the board, the other two recruits and I had had our 49 per cent grades moved up to the requisite 50 per cent. I had passed every other exam and Superintendent T.J. O'Sullivan was to be rid of me after all.

That evening, the soon-to-be banghardaí from the April classes all put on the outfits we had bought for our passing out and flounced into the corridor to show them off to each other. I saw immediately that another recruit, Ann Higgins, and I were wearing the exact same dress. We looked at each other and burst out laughing! A huddle formed at once to establish what could be done to remedy the situation. I decided to be magnanimous. 'It's okay,' I said. 'I won't wear it, I'll get something else.' I called Kitty the following day and told her what had happened. I asked whether she and my father could spare the money for a new outfit. 'Of course we'll send the money, Majella,' she said. 'It's such an important day for you.' She paused. 'I have to tell you, though, I don't think your father is going to

go down to Templemore for the graduation ceremony.'
I couldn't believe it. My heart sank. 'What?' I said,
'Why not?'

'Oh, you know Hugh,' Kitty replied. 'He said he
thinks it's too long a journey and there's no need for
him to go.'

'Typical,' I said.

It was true that my father rarely went anywhere
except on business and always complained about
having to travel any distance at all. I had thought that
he would make an exception for my graduation, that,
just this once, he might show me that he cared enough
to be there and support me. The child in me wanted to
make him proud and prove to him that I could make
something of myself. The fact that he wasn't intending
to come felt like another rejection.

Kitty and my father sent a postal order for £200,
which was so generous I felt it had to be a confirmation
that my father wouldn't be at the ceremony. He must
be feeling guilty, I thought, to have sent all that money.
I went into Templemore and bought a grey suit, gloves,
new shoes and a matching hat. When I put it all together,
I thought I looked very chic but, in retrospect, it was
terribly conservative. A ninety-year-old wouldn't wear
that outfit now.

While in the town, I went to a payphone to call
Fintan to make sure that he, *at least*, would be at the
ceremony on Thursday. Whatever happened, I knew

that I was going to have to tell him that my period still hadn't come and that there was every chance I was five weeks pregnant. Fintan, it turned out, had arranged to have the Thursday and Friday off. 'I'll be there,' he said. 'Don't you worry.'

The day before our passing out, all the recruits from April 'B', 'C' and 'D' classes were asked to come to the hall. There was huge excitement as we walked along the corridors because the rumour was that we were about to be given our placements. As far as we knew, we could be sent anywhere in the country and we would have to just pack our bags and go. We hadn't been allowed to submit any requests for preferred locations because the placements were randomly selected, or so we had been told. I was hoping to be sent to Cork. I reckoned a new life in a smaller city would suit me perfectly.

When we arrived in the hall, Superintendent T.J. O'Sullivan was standing at a lectern on the stage. As soon as we were assembled, he leaned into the microphone. 'The following is a list of the station placements for recruits from the April intake of classes,' he said, then proceeded to call out the list. As he read through the Bs, Cs and Ds I found myself wondering how Fintan had felt when he heard he was going to Donegal. I knew he had been hoping for Dublin or Cavan. Might I end up in a small rural station in a far-flung county? Eventually the superintendent reached the Ms and called out, 'Majella Moynihan, Store Street Station, Dublin.' Store Street! It wasn't Cork but nevertheless, I was delighted. I had heard that Store Street was a very busy station and a great place to learn on the job. It would be a challenging environment – which included having to deal with the slagging and the name-calling that I knew were part of the job in the big Dublin stations – but I felt I was ready for it. Now that I knew where I was going, I was so looking forward to starting my career as a guard.

The morning of our passing out, I was so excited. At breakfast, the graduands all laughed and joked with each other, relieved that the serious business of exams, results and placements was over. Now we just had to get through the parade without making fools of ourselves and then at last we could relax. It was to be a bittersweet day because we would also be saying goodbye to each other – in some cases, forever. Back in the dormitory I put on my uniform. If, as I feared, I was pregnant, there was no sign of it yet in my frame. After weeks spent running, jumping and swimming every day, I was fit and lean, with no hint of swelling in my belly. Maybe it was going to be okay? After all, I thought, I wouldn't be the first woman to have a pregnancy scare that turned out to be a false alarm. I tied the laces of my hideous shoes, put on my hat and ran to join my classmates.

The passing-out parade was wonderful. The weather

was glorious, and as we marched out I saw my family, standing together in the square. Kitty and her sisters Ann and Rita; my own sisters, all four of them; and – was it *him*? It *was* him – my father. I couldn't believe it. I was so happy. It was the most important day of my life and he was there to see it. I swung my hands, stamped my feet and saluted with extra gusto. In that moment, everything was *perfect*.

The ceremony concluded with a speech given by Minister of State at the Department of Justice, Nuala Fennell. The minister made a point of addressing the newly qualified banghardaí in the group, saying: 'If you find barriers to your advancement, deal with them. Do not accept unreal or mythical obstacles to total job fulfilment.'

I smiled at the thought of my future self, toppling barriers and leaping obstacles. Afterwards, I brought everyone for dinner to Hayes's Hotel in Thurles. It was a tradition then for newly graduated recruits to treat their guests to dinner in Hayes's. I realised it was the first time we had ever been anywhere together as a family – father, stepmother and all five sisters – outside of the orphanage or Shandon Road. Fintan was there too, making awkward conversation with my father, and telling everyone about the life of a guard in Donegal. 'Well, you know, of course, that Majella will be in Store Street,' my father retorted. 'It's a very different job up in Dublin.'

In the evening, there was dancing. My father whirled Kitty around the room for waltz after waltz and the sight of the two of them together like that made me think about my mother. What would she have been like if she had lived? What would she have thought of my new career? How might it have been to see her face in the crowd as I marched in the parade, or to treat her to dinner in a hotel? Would it have made her proud? I wondered if my father ever thought about her now or if Kitty had entirely supplanted her, in his thoughts as well as everywhere else.

I tapped my father on the shoulder and said, 'Do I get a dance?' 'You do if you want one,' he replied. We waltzed together in silence for a while and then he said, 'You've done really well for yourself, Majella. I'm very happy for you.' I smiled and he added, 'You're a great dancer. Just like your mother.'

By the end of the night, I was on such a high that I almost decided not to tell Fintan about my missed period. Part of me knew, though, that I couldn't avoid it any longer. Now that both of us had completed our training, we would have to face up to our responsibilities, whatever they might turn out to be. I'd had several anxious weeks to prepare myself for this conversation. When I shared my suspicions, Fintan reassured me it was nothing, that everything would be grand. Still, I wasn't so sure.

The following day, I took the train to Dublin. I sat

beside another girl from my class, Catherine Moran. Catherine was a brilliant, forthright Kerrywoman and the two of us had grown very close during our time in the training college. Catherine had also been assigned to Store Street and, as we journeyed together in the direction of our new lives, we reminisced about the friends we had made and thought, with excitement, about the future.

Little did I know that Superintendent T.J. O'Sullivan had sent me away with a parting gift. As I made my way to Dublin, a report he had written about me and my time in Templemore was also making its way to Store Street. I can only imagine how its contents were to shape the opinions of my superiors.

Training Record Bangharda Abina Moynihan 00338G

Bangharda Moynihan was allocated to Store Street Garda Station on the 30th of September 1983. She has very limited ability but is reluctant to use the ability which she has. She is inconsistent and immature and when counselled about her performance will readily cry. Her romantic affairs are clearly her priority. In general, Bangharda Moynihan is a very poor prospect and I doubt if she has the capacity to serve in a busy station like Store Street. She will need a lot of assistance, guidance and strict supervision, if she is to make the grade. Forward for information of her divisional and district officers, so that her progress may be very clearly monitored during periods of probation, as she is a very weak prospect.

11

Store Street

I was one of four banghardaí from my class in Templemore to be assigned to Store Street. We arrived on 30 September 1983, fresh off the train from Tipperary and full of excitement. We met with Superintendent Tommy O'Reilly, the district officer, who assigned each of us to a different unit. Store Street was a big station and had four units, with an inspector, three sergeants and twenty officers on each unit. I was assigned to Unit D, which meant that I wasn't in work until the following evening and, since none of the four of us had to go into work straight away, we decided to go across the road to Keating's pub and have a drink to celebrate the beginning of our careers. I went back to Shandon Road in the early evening and prepared my uniform and myself for work.

I was due in Store Street for parade at 5.45 p.m. the next day before my shift began at six. The parade was also known as a 'pre-tour briefing', a fifteen-minute handover during which the sergeant from the previous shift informed the incoming unit about the events of the day. At 6 p.m. sharp Sergeant Pat Dixon assigned me to a beat on O'Connell Street with another bangharda, Bridie O'Toole. I put on my tunic and walked out for my first patrol, scarcely believing that it was finally happening. I was living my dream.

It was a warm and humid evening, and as the workers and shoppers began to disperse, O'Connell Street seemed to be full of teenage boys out enjoying the sunshine. I smiled at one, who jutted his chin out at me and yelled at myself and Bridie, 'Fucking pigs.' The smile disappeared from my face as we walked on. Soon there was another shout: 'The smell of bacon off ye.' I looked at Bridie, who didn't let on that she had heard anything. I'm sure it was very naive of me but I couldn't believe that boys of that age would speak to gardaí in such a derogatory way. Still, I thought, they can call me whatever they like and I'll still be proud of myself. I'm just a happy girl to be wearing this uniform. There wasn't an insult those boys could have thrown at me that would have dampened my cheerful mood.

After four hours spent walking O'Connell Street and its environs, we headed back to the station for a break. The banghardaí had their own break room upstairs, separate from the men, where Bridie and I had a cup of tea and then we went back out again, this time to Amiens Street. We were to set up a checkpoint, and I couldn't imagine anything more exciting. There I was, standing in the middle of the road, stopping traffic, just as I had always imagined. I stopped a taxi and the driver said to me, 'Sure, you're only out of Templemore.' My confidence was rattled. The cheek of him, I thought. How could he tell that I was such a new recruit? As though reading my mind, he said, 'You look about sixteen.' I glowered at him but waved him on.

It might sound strange but those hours on the checkpoint, stopping cars and chatting to passers-by, were pure bliss for me. I floated back to Store Street when our shift was over and changed into my civilian clothes, as happy as if I had spent the night in a dance hall. I hardly slept a wink in Shandon Road, I was so exhilarated. This, at last, was happiness. This, at last, was fulfilment.

For the next few weeks I kept my head down, worked my shifts and revelled in my new life. The work was everything I had hoped it would be: absorbing, exhausting and satisfying. It was easy to focus on the job and ignore the niggling voice in my head that said I was pregnant. I spoke to Fintan on the phone every couple of days but he only ever asked how I was getting on at work, he never mentioned the conversation we had had on the day of my graduation.

Eventually, after more than eight weeks with no sign of my period, I decided it was time to take a test. On a cold Wednesday in October, an hour before I was due in for the late shift, I walked from Phibsborough into town and went to the family planning clinic on Cathal Brugha Street. I was seen by a nurse, who gave me a small container and asked me to provide a urine sample. Within minutes she had confirmed my misgivings and told me I was pregnant. At that moment, my whole world fell apart. The life I had been building for myself, the career I had wanted for as long as I could remember, every hope I had cherished for both seemed at once to be dashed by this revelation.

My instinct was to keep the news to myself. I couldn't bear the thought of telling my family – I had been doing so well and making them proud and now they would all be ashamed of me. Nor did I want to tell Fintan, who had remained silent on the subject. In that moment, I felt that if I didn't tell anybody, no one might ever know, so I went to Store Street station, got into my uniform and went out on the beat. I walked O'Connell Street that night, knowing that I was pregnant but pretending that everything was fine. On one occasion, when the strain became unbearable, I stepped off the beat and, in a little laneway, I wept.

By the following morning, I knew that I had to confide in someone. My father was out at work, so I went down to the kitchen, where Kitty was making

Eve's pudding. 'Kitty,' I said, 'there's something I have to tell you.'

Kitty was busy with her sponge and only half-listening to me but I caught her eye and she realised something was wrong. 'What is it?' she asked, full of concern. 'What's wrong?' 'Fintan and I … we, I mean … I found out that I'm …' I stammered, but couldn't go on. I leaned against the counter, feeling light-headed.

'Oh God, Majella. Oh no,' Kitty cried, putting her hand to her mouth. 'Are you pregnant?'

'I am,' I said. It was a relief to finally say it out loud.

'Are you getting married?' she asked.

'I don't know,' I replied. 'I haven't talked it over with Fintan.'

Kitty looked grave. 'Whatever you do,' she said, 'don't tell your father. We can hide it from him. If Fintan won't marry you, you can have the child adopted. But don't ever breathe a word of this to your father.'

Kitty was full of decency and compassion but she was a realist too. She knew my father would have taken the news of my pregnancy very badly, particularly in the absence of an engagement. Over the last ten months, since I had been accepted into the guards, we had become something like a happy family unit and a fragile peace had settled over Shandon Road. Kitty couldn't bear to have it shattered. Though I understood her fears in that regard, it wasn't my father's anger that scared me – we had been through all of that before and our relationship had survived – it was his coldness and indifference. I couldn't bear to be rejected by him. As a child, his abandonment of me and my sisters had caused years of hurt and pain. Now, in my vulnerable state, I couldn't go through all that again. I wanted my father's love and acceptance and I needed the security of a place to stay. So I held my tongue.

The only other person living in Shandon Road at that time was my sister Catherine. As the head of the family, Catherine had always been there if I needed her during our time in the home. I knew that I could trust my big sister so, having sworn her to secrecy, I told her about the baby. Catherine was deeply religious and was devastated, first of all, that I'd had sex outside marriage. But she was as sweet and kind-hearted as ever, her concern for my welfare trumping everything else.

I knew, of course, that I would also have to tell Fintan that my suspicions were, indeed, correct. It wasn't a conversation I wanted to have over the phone but I felt it couldn't wait any longer. I couldn't make the call from my father's house, so I walked to the nearest payphone on the Phibsborough Road and called his digs. Mrs Grayson said that Fintan was just walking out the door but I insisted that she put him on the phone. He was on his way to work and asked if our conversation could wait until later. Under pressure, I hurriedly told him about the pregnancy. There was a pause before he asked if I was sure. I confirmed that I was. 'Will you leave that with me,' he said.

Three days later, Fintan arrived at the door of Shandon Road, without notice. I was astonished to see him standing there. He told me he'd come to see my father.

'What business have you with my father?' I hissed. 'You'd better not say a word to him about the baby. If you open your mouth about it, you're dead!'

Fintan walked past me and headed for my father's room at the back of the house. I waited anxiously in the sitting room.

Twenty minutes later, Fintan came back and told me he had just asked my father for my hand in marriage. 'What did you do that for?' I asked, astounded. 'I'm not sure that I want to get married.' It was Fintan's turn to be astounded. 'Well, your father has agreed, so I think you should consider your position,' he replied. After he left, I went to my room and burst into tears.

I couldn't believe my father had agreed to Fintan's proposal. Although the two had met several times in passing, my father knew very little about Fintan and could have had no real sense of his suitability as a husband. I tried to imagine my father quizzing him about his intentions, his family and his finances but it seemed unlikely that he would have done anything of the sort. I doubted that the pair of them had engaged in anything more than chit-chat. Maybe my father had been flattered to be consulted by Fintan at all and felt that now was not the time to play the domineering patriarch. In any case, had he known I was pregnant, no doubt the conversation would have taken a very different tone.

I knew that marrying Fintan was what a girl in my position was supposed to do. Now that he had spoken to my father and proposed to me, I felt a huge pressure to do what I knew would be regarded as the right thing. It would certainly solve all my problems. If we married quickly, no one would mind too much if the baby arrived a few months early. That could all be explained away. I suspected, too, that the guards would respond much better to the news of my pregnancy if I had a ring on my finger and a man in my life. But there were other facts to consider.

For starters, I was only twenty-one years old and in truth I wasn't sure that I loved Fintan enough to spend the rest of our lives together and, in a country where divorce was still illegal, that was a very big qualm indeed. In the end, it came down to the fact that, if Fintan and I were married, I would be able to keep the baby. I had always wanted to be a mother and, even if the circumstances weren't quite what I had imagined, the chance was too great to pass up, I called Fintan and said, 'Okay, it's a maybe.'

'A maybe, Majella?' he replied.

'All right, it's a yes. I do think it would be better if we were married.'

Fintan said he would come to Dublin as soon as he could. And that was it. No ring, no romantic proposal or acceptance, and yet I was engaged. Now that it was settled, I began to contemplate our future. Where would we live? Would I transfer to Donegal or would Fintan move to Dublin? If he came to work in Store Street, would we get on each other's nerves? With our two salaries, could we afford a house? There was so much to consider. I could also begin to think of our baby with anticipation instead of fear. I wondered if it was a boy or a girl and whether Fintan had a preference. I started to make a list of names I liked. Danielle, I thought, if it's a girl. And maybe Fintan for a boy?

The following evening, when I came into work in Store Street I got a message to say that I'd had a phone call from a Mrs Casey. I only knew one Mrs Casey and that was Fintan's mother. I didn't want to speak to her in the station, so I waited until the following day to call her back from Shandon Road. She wanted to arrange to speak to my father about the wedding, as it was vital the ceremony was arranged before my condition became apparent. 'What concern is it of yours?' I asked. 'That's between myself and Fintan.'

The dignity of her family was her concern, she explained, and she advised that my father had a right to know and that I must tell him about the baby. 'Fair enough,' I said, an audible quiver in my voice. 'I'll tell him.'

I was nervous that Fintan's mother might tell my father that I was pregnant before I'd plucked up the courage to tell him myself. I decided to wait until the next time that Fintan came down to visit, so that we could tell him together. But when Fintan came back to Shandon Road, ten days later, a conversation with my father was the very last thing on his mind. He told me as soon as we were alone that he was not prepared for marriage and a child. It took me a moment to understand what he was saying. When I did, I was hit with a wave of terror. 'What are you going to do?' I asked, feeling sick. 'Are you just going to walk away?' He repeated what he had told me, and added that his mother was questioning whether or not he was the father. I could not believe what I was hearing.

Fintan left the house, leaving me in a state of panic.

We spoke one last time after that. I was at St. Vincent's Hospital visiting the girls in St. Rita's, and I called the house in Donegal to establish, once and for all, what his intentions were. But the conversation only confirmed my worst fears. It was clear to me that Fintan had washed his hands of the situation. I was well and truly on my own.

12

Telling the guards

By mid-December, I was almost four months pregnant. I was young, it was my first pregnancy and stress had curbed my usually hearty appetite, so I was skinnier than ever and no one would have guessed by looking at me that I was carrying a child.

I was still living with my father and stepmother in the house in Shandon Road. Kitty was being as attentive as she could be, without drawing attention to my condition – making my meals and washing and ironing my uniform. Together, we kept my pregnancy a secret from my father. It wasn't always easy: I suffered from terrible nausea in the mornings and spent the first twenty minutes of every day vomiting in the bathroom. Fortunately, my father's bedroom and the reception rooms were downstairs, so he never heard a thing.

At no point in my pregnancy – at least, not until the very end – did I consult a doctor or a midwife. I was never advised by anyone to do so. Kitty had never had children of her own, so she knew nothing about the correct procedure, and the subject never came up in the family planning clinic. It simply didn't occur to me to see anyone, so I didn't.

I knew I was going to have to tell the guards that I was pregnant but I had no idea how to go about doing so. What was the protocol in these matters? The idea of informing my superiors was intimidating and I had no idea how they were likely to respond. Sometimes I assumed I would be fired at once, while at other times I imagined they might react with compassion and empathy. I soothed myself with the idea that I might have underestimated the organisation entirely. After all, I was a member of An Garda Síochána, one of their own. Surely the least I could expect from them was loyalty?

The family planning clinic had referred me to CURA, a crisis pregnancy support agency that was affiliated with the Catholic Church. Shortly before Christmas I presented myself at the CURA offices in Marlborough Street, where the social worker was a woman by the name of Mena Robinson. I introduced myself to Mena and told her about my predicament and immediately found her to be very kind and supportive. She made me a cup of tea and listened to my hopes and fears. I told her I was a guard and that I was afraid to approach the authorities because I didn't want to lose my job. She told me to leave all that in her hands, that she would arrange a meeting for me with An Garda Síochána and smooth things over as much as she could. I was relieved and thanked her profusely. As I got up to leave, Mena said, 'I should tell you, Majella, that I also run an organisation called The Rotunda Girls Aid Society, and should you choose to go down that route I will be in a position to find a lovely family for your baby. A family who would love a child so much.' I thanked her and promised to give the matter some thought.

Mena arranged for a female inspector from my unit to meet with me in the CURA offices a fortnight later. Although we had shared a workplace for months, she was a senior bangharda and I was only on nodding terms with her. I certainly had no idea as to the level of pastoral care she was willing to provide to her junior colleagues.

The fact that we were meeting in the headquarters of a crisis pregnancy agency must have given the inspector some indication of the matter at hand but when, after some preliminary chat, I told her I was expecting a child, she was aghast, particularly when I added that I was not likely to be getting married anytime soon. Any fantasies I might have entertained about solidarity or empathy were quickly dispelled, when she coldly responded with 'You know that you are a recruit?' The meaning of the question was lost on me at that moment – I was more concerned about the complete lack of compassion in her voice. 'Maybe,' Mena interjected, 'you could give Majella a sense of what might happen next in the station.' 'Honestly, Mena, I haven't a clue,' she replied. 'This has never happened before in Store Street.' She turned to me with a somewhat antagonistic look, as though reminded of the fact that I was the first to step out of line. 'You will have to tell your district officer,' she said. Then, after I promised to do everything she asked, one final question: 'What are you going to do with the child?' I told her that I didn't know.

I was telling the absolute truth when I said I hadn't decided what to do about the baby. A consensus was already forming, at that early stage, to the effect that it would be unwise for me to keep it. Kitty felt that the whole affair should remain a secret; Mena felt that the child would have much better prospects if he or she was placed with a family, and the inspector seemed to regard the pregnancy as a blot on my character and my career. Despite the pressure I was already beginning to feel to have my baby adopted, I balked at the idea. How could I, who had suffered so much pain and hurt because of my father's rejection of me, now reject my son or daughter in turn? How could I betray my own innocent little infant? And yet the alternative seemed to be isolation, stigma, and – if I was to lose my job – poverty. I couldn't contemplate either outcome, so I avoided making any decision at all, save one: that I would not, under any circumstances, have an abortion. Despite my many doubts and fears, I never once considered going to England. I was going to give birth to the baby and that was that.

The meeting with the female inspector had been disillusioning and rather ominous as an indicator of the likely reaction of An Garda Síochána. At the very least, though, it meant that I had begun the process of telling the guards about my pregnancy, so I pressed on, hopeful that her response might only represent that of one individual inspector and not that of the entire organisation.

A few weeks later, in January 1984, I met with the district officer, Superintendent Tommy O'Reilly, in Store Street. The female inspector had suggested that all three of us sit down together, but since she wasn't likely to be much help, I had made an appointment with Tommy for myself alone. I had met the superintendent on my first day in the station and he had seemed to me like a decent man, so I thought I would try my luck with him. We met in his office at 6 p.m. one evening, at the end of my shift, and I blurted out the words, 'Superintendent O'Reilly, I'm pregnant, Sir.' Silence. I waited, anxiously, for his reply, knowing that my career might well hang in the balance. 'Who,' he asked, 'is the father of the child?' I was taken aback by the question. The fact that he was my superior didn't give the superintendent the right to pry into my personal life. After all, what difference did it make to him who the father was? Before I had a chance to gather myself, Tommy O'Reilly asked again, 'Who is the father? Is he a guard?' I didn't seem to have any option, other than to answer, 'He is.' Tommy then took out a pen and paper and said, 'Tell me his name.' I remember asking, 'Why is it so important who he is and whether or not he's a guard?' 'Well,' said Tommy, 'he's a recruit and you're a recruit.' I didn't know what he meant by that. Then he asked me how far along I was. 'Twenty weeks,' I replied. And that was that.

The following day, Tommy O'Reilly approached me after parade and told me I was to be taken in from the street for my own safety. I was no longer to go on the beat and would instead be working in the collator's office.

Though I was aware that, in certain respects, it was a punishment to be removed from normal duties, I was also quite excited to work in that office. The collator's official title was criminal intelligence officer and his job was to compile the reported movements of suspects and known criminals as recorded by officers on patrol. These details were often quite innocuous – what car a person drove, for example, where they lived or with whom they were known to associate – but they were all filed away and accessed when a crime was committed in order to confirm an alibi or build a case against an individual. The office turned out to be a haven for me. I loved the work and the two men who were in there, the collator and his assistant, were perfect gentlemen. In all the time we worked together, neither one ever made the slightest reference to the fact I was pregnant.

Elsewhere in Store Street, however, things weren't so pleasant. The rumour mill had swung into action and I had become the station's main subject of gossip. My friend Catherine Moran, who had been in my class in Templemore, told me that it was widely known that I was pregnant, that the other guards in the station regularly speculated as to when I was due, how big I was likely to get and whether I would eventually be given the sack. Catherine also said that she was often asked about the identity of the child's father and said that the suspicion was that he might also be a guard. Always loyal and trustworthy, Catherine never revealed a single detail.

As well as the chatter behind my back, I also felt that I was treated differently in the station, particularly by the senior officers. All indications were that I was regarded by many of them as a troublemaker and whenever I was in a room with any of them the atmosphere was often cold and hostile. My working day began to be interrupted by regular summonses to the offices of various inspectors, who would quiz me about my pregnancy and my intentions for the baby's future. Those men – and they were all men – felt they had the right to know anything at all about my private life and my personal affairs. If they asked me a question, they felt it was my duty to answer it.

Although I found those conversations unpleasant, I received no indication from any of my superiors that my career was in jeopardy. I thought I was safe in my job and that after I gave birth I would be allowed to come back to work with no repercussions. Of course, I was wrong. I didn't know it then, but shortly after I reported my pregnancy to Superintendent Tommy O'Reilly he passed on the information to the chief superintendent of the Dublin Metropolitan Area. I would later read the redacted communication in my garda file.

Training Record – R. Ban/Garda Abina M. Moynihan, 00338G, Store Street

On January 16, 1984, Recruit Ban Garda Moynihan informed me that she is pregnant. As she was in her 17th week, I placed her on indoor duties.

I understand the circumstances to be as follows. For more than two years she had been keeping company with Fintan Casey.

Moynihan passed out on the 30.9.1983.

Between those dates, she visited Donegal while on week-end passes, and on one of those visits conception took place.

At this time her intention is to have the baby adopted.

Ban Garda Moynihan arrived here from the Training Centre on the 30.9.83. From that date she was subjected to normal recruit supervision. However, on the 2.11.1983, she was placed in the special supervision category. This entailed special periodic reports from her supervisors.

She has fitted in well here since she came. She is honest, dependable, and willing. She has been active in her duties and has not been found wanting in assertiveness and courage on the street. Though pressed hard by me in my interview with her on her behaviour in the Training Centre, she did not resort to tears.

I am particularly impressed by her devotion to duty while pregnant. She did not seek special duties and went out on duty on occasions while feeling unwell. She is now employed in the Collator's office and has impressed the sergeant there with her ability and enthusiasm for work.

I consider, at this point, that she will make an efficient member of the force.

T.J. O'Reilly
Superintendent

As a result of this letter, lines of communication opened up which went all the way to the highest echelons of An Garda Síochána, discussing me and my pregnancy. On 22 February Michael Bohan, the personal assistant to the garda commissioner, sent a short communiqué to Store Street.

Re: R/Ban Garda Abina M. Moynihan, 00338G, Store Street Garda Station, D.M.A.

Please report further when baby is born to above-named.

13

A guarded secret

In February, Superintendent Tommy O'Reilly called me into his office. 'When is your baby due, Majella?' he asked. I was weary from weeks of questioning and I could feel my eyes fill with tears. 'Around the 21st of May, Superintendent.'

'There's no cause for getting upset,' he barked. 'We just need to arrange your maternity leave.'

I was relieved and surprised. I had become so caught up in the humiliation and shame associated with my pregnancy that I had hardly given a moment's thought to more practical considerations.

Tommy O'Reilly told me that I was entitled to fourteen weeks' maternity leave and that my 'confinement', as it was termed, would commence two months before the baby was due. That seemed very early and I wondered if the haste wasn't owing to a desire to get me out of the station before I became too big to ignore – even though it was clear that everyone knew. But I said nothing and filled out the half-sheet that was presented to me to provide a report of my pregnancy. This was to be passed along to the Office of the Chief Superintendent in Harcourt Street, for his signoff. Once that was done, I was informed that, in six weeks' time, I would be expected to take my leave.

Now that I had begun to make arrangements for the future, it soon occurred to me how much I still had to organise. I had hardly considered the fact that, whether I decided to keep the baby or not, one way or another, I would be giving birth in May. I had no idea where that was going to happen or how to go about securing a bed in a maternity hospital. Most pressing of all was the fact that I was still living in Shandon Road, under the roof of a man who had no idea that I was pregnant. If my condition was to remain a secret from my father, I needed new accommodation and I needed it urgently. I called into Mena Robinson in CURA and told her my predicament. Mena spoke to her network of colleagues around the country and within days a social worker in Galway had found a family who were known to care for young, unmarried women who had got themselves 'into trouble'. It was arranged that I would stay with this family for the final months of my pregnancy before giving birth in Galway Regional Hospital.

My maternity leave began at the end of March. There were no goodbyes when I finished up in Store Street; nobody wished me luck and there was no cake or card. I just quietly packed away my things and then I disappeared.

I was almost seven months pregnant and only just beginning to show when I left my father's house in Phibsborough and got a bus to Kilnaleck in Cavan. My sister Anne, knowing what lay ahead of me, had invited me to stay with her family for a fortnight before I went on to Galway for my confinement.

Kitty and I had agreed that we would tell my father I was off on a temporary transfer to a garda station in Connemara for a few months. As I was leaving the house, he wished me the best of luck and asked me to write to him to tell him how I was getting on. 'I will of course,' I said.

On the bus to Cavan I began to feel unwell, and by the time I reached Kilnaleck I was crippled with pain. Anne called a local GP, Dr. John Sullivan, who came to the house and took a urine sample, suspecting that I was suffering from a kidney infection. Dr. Sullivan was surprised to learn that he was the first doctor I had consulted throughout my pregnancy, so he carried out an antenatal examination, on the basis of which he inferred that my own estimated due date was indeed correct, 21 May. He called the following day to confirm that I was suffering from a urinary tract infection and recommended that I take fluid and aspirin for the pain. I thought very little about that doctor and I doubt he thought very much about me, until he was later called to testify to a sworn inquiry of An Garda Síochána.

*

My sister Anne and I had never had a very deep relationship prior to those weeks in 1984. We had spent very little time under the same roof. She had left St. Joseph's seven years before I did and, by the time I moved to Shandon Road, in 1980, Anne was long gone. And yet, when I was in trouble and needed a place to stay, my sister took me in and treated me with kindness, love and respect. She had three children of her own to think of: Brian, who was eight, Shane, who was seven and Julie, the baby, who was just a year old. I loved being around them all and I doted on Julie, who was a beautiful little thing. It was very affecting, almost painful, to be sharing a house with an infant at that point in my pregnancy. I didn't know, then, whether I was having a boy or a girl and I found myself looking at my niece and imagining my own daughter and myself as a mother. By the time I left Cavan, I was more confused than ever.

The bus journey to Galway was the most lonely and desolate of my life. Anne had made sandwiches for me and a flask of tea but I was so distraught that I left them both behind. It felt so wrong, at that time of all times, to be leaving my family to go and spend weeks in the company of strangers. The expectation, from almost everyone who knew about my pregnancy, was that I was going away to give birth and that I would then give the baby to a family, so that I could re-emerge in society as though nothing at all had happened. I didn't see how that could be possible. How could any young woman carry a child within her body for nine months and not be changed forever by the experience? How could a mother hand over her newborn infant and then pretend that no such person had ever existed?

I still hadn't decided what I was going to do about my baby. For more than seven months, I had avoided making any kind of plan for the child's future, hoping that circumstances might change in a way that would allow me to keep him or her. But my circumstances were precisely the same in March 1984 as they had been in October 1983: I was twenty-one years old, I was living in my father's house and I was working for An Garda Síochána. Everyone – the guards, CURA, even Kitty – seemed to regard adoption as the one acceptable course of action. Fintan was my only lifeline and I hadn't heard from him since that last, terrible phone call. It seemed like a lost cause.

Mary Cannon, the woman of the house, collected me at the bus station and drove me to her family's farm in Ardrahan. She lived there in a two-storey farmhouse with her husband Michael John and their three young children, Seán, Liam and Elaine. I felt like an alien arriving in their home and I was embarrassed in front of the children, who were only twelve, eleven and four years old. I wondered what Mary and Michael John said to them about me and the other girls who came to stay. Still, they all did their utmost to make me feel welcome. They brought me on a tour of the house and farm before we sat down to tea.

Mary, who was then in her early forties, was warm and caring: a quintessential Irish mammy. She kept her house clean and tidy and cooked the most wonderful meals. She never told me why she took pregnant girls into her home – I think it was just in her nature to help people. She was religious, but without a trace of sanctimony, and I felt that she had a genuine care for young women who were in trouble.

The day after I arrived, the social worker who had arranged my stay called at the house. Her name was also Mary and she was from the Galway branch of CURA. From our first meeting, all of the talk was about adoption. Mary assumed that it was my intention to have the baby adopted as soon as possible. 'After all,' she said, 'you're only twenty-one and you're on your own. It would be better if the child went to a good family.' She told me that she already had the perfect couple lined up, who were longing for a son or daughter of their own, and she would ensure that the process would be as smooth as possible. She arranged to come to the farmhouse once a week to check on my progress.

Looking back, it seems so inappropriate, so unseemly and so wrong that no one ever sat me down and talked through my needs and wants in relation to my child. No one ever discussed how I might have gone about keeping the baby, or what our allowances and entitlements would have been if I decided to do so. After all, I may have been a very young woman but I was a young woman with qualifications and a job. The idea that I might raise a child on my own was not such a ludicrous one. Yet it was assumed by everyone I spoke to that they knew what was best for me and my baby and what was best was adoption. Nor did anyone explain what exactly was involved in giving a child up for adoption and what rights I would and would not retain if I went down that route. It felt as though everyone had agreed that I was producing this child to give to more suitable people than myself and that the less contact we had after that, the better.

The farm was less than two miles outside Kinvara. For the first few days I walked into the village every morning but I quickly discerned that more than one person there had heard about 'the pregnant guard from Dublin'. Everywhere I went I got the sense that I was being pitied or reviled. I began to avoid Kinvara altogether and instead spent my days out roaming the country roads around the farm or walking Traught beach.

Mary Cannon involved me in everything. She treated me as though I was one of the family. When she and Michael John went out, I would look after the children. When Mary went to visit her mother and father, she'd bring me with her. We often went into Galway city, and Mary would take me to Ryan's for some shopping and then we'd go for coffee together. Or she'd bring me out for the day to Salthill or Connemara.

We went to mass in Galway Cathedral, and I remember feeling so vulnerable and self-conscious with my big bump in my third trimester, as we listened to Bishop Eamonn Casey preach about the 'disappointment and disapproval' that Christians were justified in feeling towards unmarried mothers. I felt that everyone in the cathedral could tell that I was one of those women. Of course it would later be discovered that Bishop Casey had himself fathered a child with a single woman, but in 1984 his secret was safe and he had no compunction about declaring that unmarried mothers could remain 'closer to God' if they gave their babies up for adoption.

When Mary heard that I hadn't been seeing a doctor in Dublin, she was appalled, and insisted on taking me to her GP for a check-up. Dr. Pat agreed with the due date that Dr. John Sullivan had fixed on during the examination in Cavan, then he checked my bump and said that, as far as he was concerned, the baby was doing just fine.

Still, despite all Mary's kindness, I felt strange and out of place. At dinner, the family were often joined by the men who worked out in the fields with Michael John. I was young and gaunt and vulnerable and, whenever the men were around, I had the uncomfortable feeling that I was being watched. I began to avoid those gatherings as much as possible and ate dinner alone in my room. At night I slept fitfully. Several times every night I would wake and walk around the bedroom, fretting about my baby and the future in the guards.

I decided to phone my sergeant in Templemore, Dan Corrigan, who had always been so kind to us all. Dan had given each of us recruits his telephone number on the day of our graduation and told us that, if we ever needed anything, we could give him a call. I rang him and told him I was pregnant, and was so happy when he responded with compassion and concern for my welfare. It was unusual to speak to a member of An Garda Síochána about my pregnancy and have them ask how I was doing. I was glad I called him.

The following week Dan and his wife Nora and their daughter arrived at the house in Kinvara to take me out to dinner. It was a very kind gesture at a time when I felt so isolated within the guards. During the meal I asked Dan if he thought the pregnancy would be a problem for my career in the future, whether it was something the guards might hold against me. He said he simply didn't know because he had never known of an unmarried bangharda to become pregnant before.

'I can't possibly be the first in twenty-four years,' I said, amazed.

'I'm sure there were others, Majella,' he said.

Dan wasn't my only visitor while I was in Galway. My friend Catherine Moran often came from Dublin to tell me all the news from Store Street. I asked Catherine what was being said about me in the station. 'The older guards are gossiping like aul' ones,' she said, 'and they're all calling you "easy". But the younger guards are supportive.' Catherine herself was always very good to me. She knew that the pregnancy had come as a shock but she never presumed I wanted to give up the baby. Catherine always said I could come and live in her house with the child if I decided to keep it.

Kitty came down several times with her sisters Ann and Rita, and I was always delighted to see them. We usually drove out to Dunguaire Castle on the shore of Galway Bay to go for a walk. They brought parcels of food and clothes, and as they were leaving, each of the sisters in turn would hold my hand in hers and tell me to mind myself.

There was one visit, though, that chilled and unnerved me. It was from my unit inspector who had spoken to Mena Robinson earlier in my pregnancy. She arrived at the farmhouse towards the end of May, ostensibly to see how I was doing. Mary Cannon led her into the good room and brought tea and biscuits, then left us to talk.

It quickly became clear, however, that the inspector hadn't come all the way to Galway for chit-chat. She began pumping me for information, which I assumed was to be relayed back to Store Street and beyond. She asked what I planned to do with the baby, whether it would be given up for adoption. She asked whether there was a chance myself and Fintan might still marry. It was question after question, as though we were in her office in Store Street and I had just committed a crime. I responded truthfully and to the best of my ability. I felt I had no other choice. When she was satisfied that her questions had been answered, she looked at me and said, 'I hope you know, Majella, that your behaviour, as a recruit, has brought great discredit on the guards.' I was stunned. 'I'm so sorry,' I said. Although I didn't understand how my own personal crisis could have affected the organisation so deeply, I knew that I felt dirty and ashamed.

She left shortly afterwards and I walked back to

my bedroom, crushed. That was the first time that I was accused of bringing discredit on the guards. But it wouldn't be the last.

14

A beautiful boy

Having been told that my due date was 21 May, I thought, in my innocence, that that would be the day I would give birth. But the day passed, and the following day and the day after that, with no sign at all of the baby's arrival. Those days were hellish. My belly felt heavy and my back ached but all that was nothing compared with the mental anguish I was suffering. I was still full of doubt over what to do with my child. At times I thought that once the baby was out and in my arms, I would find the strength to keep him or her. At other times I just wanted the whole ordeal to be over and to go back to my normal life. I felt insecure and frightened and completely alone. I didn't know where to turn.

In order to stop the process that had begun the moment I contacted CURA in Dublin – that is, the process of taking my child from me and giving him or her to another family to be adopted – I would have needed to be strong-willed, self-assured and certain that the course of action I was taking was the right one. But I was none of those things. For months I had been told by my stepmother, by An Garda Síochána and by CURA that the best thing for my family, for my career and above all for my baby would be to have the child adopted. Who was I to stand up to all that? Especially now that CURA was telling me they had a couple who were ready and waiting. It felt as though the baby and I were on a conveyor belt and the only possible outcome was our separation.

Much of my time during those days was spent crying and reliving my childhood, dwelling on the feelings of rejection and abandonment that had stayed with me through all those years. Would my child be haunted by those same feelings if he or she was adopted? My only distraction was to go out walking or cycling the roads around Ardrahan. Sometimes Liam Cannon, Mary's second son, would accompany me, which I loved. Liam was a little dote – he was so sweet-natured and gentle. The two of us would go out on bikes together, me with my big belly, and Liam would tell me all about what was going on in school. Once, he confided to me that he hated learning the piano, even though it was his mother's dearest wish that he would.

By 27 May I was almost a week overdue and feeling very anxious. It was a Sunday and Michael John had no work to do on the farm, so he suggested that we all go out for a drive to see if that might bring on my labour. The six of us bundled into the car and off we went. Michael John drove at speed over every bump in the road between Ardrahan and Clarinbridge but I didn't feel so much as a twinge.

On the morning of the 30th, nine days after my due date, I took four tablespoons of castor oil. The thick, yellow liquid tasted vile but she said it was known to bring on labour. Whether it was the castor oil or just that my time had come, I'll never know, but sure enough, at eight o'clock that evening, my contractions started. I had never attended an antenatal class, so I knew nothing about childbirth and hadn't known to expect this terrible, frightening pain. The next few hours were a blur. My only memory is of Liam looking in at me as I screamed on my bed and Mary saying to him, 'In another while, Liam, we'll have a baby.' At midnight, she brought me into Galway Regional Hospital.

By the time we arrived at the hospital the pain was ferocious. I was ushered up to the labour ward and given a pelvic exam to measure my dilation. Six centimetres. The midwife looked down at me as I huffed and moaned through the labour spasms and asked Mary, 'Is she married?' Mary shook her head and the midwife's mouth tightened.

'Will you give her an epidural?' Mary asked.

'No,' said the midwife, 'she doesn't need it.'

In lieu of pain relief she told me to walk up and down the corridor. I held on to the wall and cried out in agony.

After an hour they brought me into the delivery room. Mary held my hand the whole time. It was a very difficult birth. I remember crying out as I was ripped apart. Then, at one minute past half five in the morning, on the feast of the Ascension, I gave birth to a baby boy. His little face was so beautiful that as soon as I caught a glimpse of him I burst into tears. He was crying too and I longed to hold him close to me, to feel his heart beat against mine. But we weren't given so much as a moment together. There was no joyful introduction; he wasn't put onto my chest and there was no skin-to-skin contact. As soon as he was out in the world the midwife whisked him away. He was put into a little trolley and taken off to another room and all I could do was watch him go.

The doctor told me that David's delivery had caused extensive tearing and that I would require at least ten stitches. I lay on the birthing bed and hardly heard a word he said. I thought of nothing but my little boy. I was filled with a loneliness and a longing I had never experienced before.

Once I had been sewn back together I was sent to the maternity ward to rest. In the ward I was surrounded by mothers with their infants. My body was telling me that I had given birth and yet I had no baby. I was exhausted and sore. My breasts were full of milk; I should have been feeding my son but he was nowhere to be seen. I lay in that bed all day and my little boy wasn't brought in to me once.

In the evening the registrar came in and asked what the child's name was. I told her I was calling him David after the Star of David. I had decided several months earlier that if I had a boy, David would be his name. I thought it was a beautiful name. I knew that, for me, my son would be a guiding star and I hoped that, for everyone else, he would be a light in the world. I heard later that the priest in the hospital had baptised him as 'David', but even though I was in the maternity ward at the time I wasn't informed or invited to attend the christening.

The following morning I called Mary. 'I'm checking myself out,' I told her. 'I can't stay here for another minute.' Mary told me that she would come in and collect me. In the meantime I decided to look for David. I had to see him again. I found the nursery on the second floor. Through the big glass window, I spotted my baby's name on his little cot and saw him inside it. I approached the nurse at her station and said, 'I'm that little boy's mother and I was wondering if I could go in and hold him.'

'Who is your son?' she asked.

'David Moynihan,' I told her.

'Oh, no,' she said, after checking her clipboard, 'you can't.'

I assumed then that CURA had informed the hospital that my baby was to be adopted, and I was heartbroken. I wanted to go in and grab David and run but I didn't know where to run to. Not home; not the guards; not my old job in Saint Vincent's – I would never have been taken back to Saint Rita's as a single mother; not Café Angelo, where I never would have made enough money to rent a place on my own. There was nowhere I could go with my baby, so I stood and looked at him through the window for as long as I could and eventually I just walked away.

I got dressed and sat on my bed and waited for Mary. The paracetamol and diclofenac that I had been given that morning had started to wear off and the pain from my stitches was excruciating. When Mary arrived and saw the state I was in she gave me a hug. 'Link my arm,' she said, and I did. I leaned on Mary as I walked out of that hospital and left my son behind. I was broken, just broken. My experience at Galway Regional was like a factory, where women came in, gave birth, dropped their babies and went. I had come in with a baby and was leaving without one.

I walked to the car park in a trance, I didn't know who I was or what I was. My mind and body felt as though they had been severed from each other. My mind was still in the hospital with my child, even as my body was climbing into the back of Mary's car and being driven away. Every nerve, every muscle, every sinew felt as though they were crying out for the baby I was leaving behind.

As we drove into Galway city, I noticed there were guards on every street, walking in groups, directing the traffic, peering into every car. It was like a nightmare. 'Why are there so many guards?' I asked Mary.

'Haven't you heard?' she replied cheerfully. 'Ronald Reagan is in Galway today.'

I hadn't heard. I cowered in the back seat, hoping that none of them would see me. I couldn't bear the thought of being recognised, that day of all days.

When we arrived at the farmhouse, I got into bed and cried and cried.

15

CURA cares

On the morning of my twenty-second birthday, ten days after David was born, Mary from CURA rang Mary Cannon. She said she was bringing David to his foster home and that they would stop by for a visit on the way. When I heard that David was coming, I felt numb. I hadn't seen him since I left the hospital and I had never once held him. No one had told me that he might come to visit, so I had stopped expecting to see him at all.

Now that the wheels of David's adoption were in motion, now that he had been taken from me and been kept away for over a week, it felt as if I had no choice but to give him up. In fact, until I signed his adoption papers, which I had not yet done, I could take him back at any time. But I believed what I had been repeatedly told, that it would be selfish to try to raise him myself unless I was certain I had a stable job and the means to keep a roof over both our heads.

To bring a child into the world only to hand that child over to the custody of others felt strange and unnatural to me. I longed for my son – to hold him in my arms, to feed him and bathe him and care for him. And yet, at the same time, I feared his presence because it could only ever be temporary. How could I allow myself to feel all the love and joy and pride I knew I felt for my little baby, if that baby couldn't stay with me? How would I carry on after he was gone? How would I retain my sanity?

Mary arrived with David within the hour. I was still in my dressing gown and sitting in the front room when the doorbell rang. Mary Cannon went out to answer the door and, when she came back in, she was carrying David. As soon as I saw him, I forgot every fear I'd had about the visit. I was mesmerised by him, adoring. I remember stroking his face with my hand and saying, 'Oh my God, you're the image of your father.' And he was – the absolute image of Fintan – the same broad nose and red hair. If only Fintan had been there, I felt certain that he would have accepted that child on sight and things might have turned out very differently.

I sat down on the couch and Mary Cannon placed David in my arms. As I held him, I felt a powerful sense of relief: that I was finally holding him; that he was mine at last; that the loneliness and yearning of the last ten days were over. Mary Cannon took a photograph of the two of us together. In the photo, I'm sitting in profile, in my dressing gown with David clasped tight to my chest. I'm staring at him and smiling but my eyes are filled with tears, some of which have fallen onto the baby's head. A photo of a new mother and her infant son should convey happiness and joy but that photo portrays nothing but a grieving woman holding a child to whom she was a stranger.

Mary explained to me what was involved in foster care. She told me that an organisation called Clarecare, who were affiliated with St. Catherine's Adoption Society, had found a woman in Ennis who would be willing to look after David temporarily, before he was placed with his adoptive family. Since the couple who were hoping to adopt David lived in Ennis too, it was felt that this set-up would ensure the smoothest possible transition for the baby. Mary told me that David's foster mother might be amenable to the idea of me visiting David but I would have to run it by his new social worker, a Sr. Mary Lillis.

Mary said then that she and the baby would have to go, as David's foster mother was expecting him. They had only been in the house for half an hour and I couldn't believe they were leaving so soon. I clutched onto David, not wanting to let him go, but Mary took him out of my hands, brought him out the door, placed him in a car-seat in the back of her car and then drove him away. Once again, I could only watch him go.

I decided to stay with Mary Cannon in Galway for another few weeks. My maternity leave wasn't due to finish for a while and I wanted to be as close to Ennis as possible, on the off-chance that I might be able to visit my son. The Cannons were kind enough to allow me to stay on and Mary offered to drive me anywhere I needed to go. She really didn't have to do all that she did for me – her kindness knew no bounds. In those weeks of instability and turmoil, that woman saved my life.

A few days after David's visit, Sr. Mary Lillis rang to introduce herself. She gave me the address of the foster mother in Ennis and told me I was welcome to call in and see him. Before we went, Mary Cannon brought me into Galway and I bought clothes and a little teddy bear to give David when I saw him.

David's foster mother, Biddy, lived in a small house right in the centre of Ennis. She was a tiny, dark-haired woman in her sixties, and from the very first time we met she couldn't have been more warm or welcoming. She had been a foster mother for many years and had a wonderful way with children. She clearly loved David and delighted in telling me about his feeding routine and how well he was sleeping. She described him as 'a sweet boy with beautiful eyes' and said that he was 'a pure pet'. Biddy told me that the first day David had arrived she had dressed him up in a little scout costume and she showed me a photo she had taken of him in the outfit. As soon as I looked at it I noticed the glint the baby had in his eyes. Oh my God, I thought, you're definitely my son. 'You can take that photo away with you,' said Biddy. I still have it to this day.

Mary Cannon and I stayed with Biddy and David for more than an hour and a half. When we were leaving, Biddy told me I was welcome to visit again soon. I cried the whole way back to Galway. 'I don't know what to do,' I sobbed to Mary. 'I want him back. What will I do?' Mary was thoughtful.

'I could take him,' she said slowly. 'Would you feel better if I took him?'

At first I thought this was a wonderful idea: if Mary had David, I could come and visit him all the time and watch him grow up. It wouldn't be the same as keeping him myself but it might be the next best thing. But then, I was filled with jealousy at the idea of Mary having my child. Would it be any better to see my son being raised by a family I knew than by a carefully vetted family of strangers? I couldn't decide, so I said nothing and I never followed up on Mary's suggestion.

*

12th June, 1984

Dear Majella,
I was so sorry to miss you the day you were down in Ennis. Anyway, I know you found your way to Bid's and hope you got on alright. David gets more beautiful all the time – if that's possible. Bid told me that you're coming again next week so I'll try my best to be here – either next Wednesday or Thursday, isn't it? Be sure and ring me beforehand and you can leave a message. Bid said you were a 'most beautiful girl' – now there's praise for you!! You made a great impression. I'm sure she did too because she's marvellous to mind babies.
Looking forward to meeting you next week, Majella.
Best wishes,
Mary Lillis (Sr.)
Social Worker

For the next three weeks, I visited David twice a week in Biddy's house. Those weeks were wonderful. I bonded with my son in a way I never thought possible and I felt he knew who I was and was comforted by my presence. But that happy time couldn't last. I got a call from Sr. Mary Lillis to say David would be moving in with his prospective adoptive parents in July and that, once he was with them, my visits would have to stop. Before that happened, it was arranged that I would meet the couple, Maeve and Desmond, so that I could get a sense of the people who were hoping to raise my son.

We met in Clarecare, in Ennis. Mary Cannon drove me down and left me at the door. As I got out of the car, she said, 'I'll be waiting for you right here when you're finished' and gave my arm a squeeze. Inside, Sr. Mary Lillis brought me through to the back of the building, where there were rooms for meetings of this nature. 'You'll like Maeve and Desmond,' she said as we walked. 'They're a lovely couple. Such good people.'

The two of them were already in the room when I arrived, sitting in grey squashy chairs, with a small table in front of them for tea. Maeve and Desmond both stood up, and looked very uncomfortable as we were introduced. Maeve took my hand in both of hers as she shook it nervously. I never discussed with them how I had come to have David or why exactly I was giving him up, but certain references they made to me and to my job indicated that they were aware I was an unmarried bangharda who couldn't keep her baby and that I had been jilted by the baby's father. I assumed Sr. Mary Lillis had been filling them in.

What I remember most vividly about that meeting was that I cried the whole way through it. At one point, possibly to console me, Desmond asked me what fears I had. 'I'm afraid of the dark and I'm afraid of water,' I said. 'Well,' replied Desmond, 'I can promise you

David won't be afraid of the dark and he won't be afraid of water.' Maeve agreed, adding that they would always love David as though he was their own and that they would always keep me informed about his life by sending letters and photos as often as possible. And with that, the meeting was over.

Outside, Mary Cannon was waiting for me, as promised. She brought me to a little pub, off the main thoroughfare in Ennis, and watched me drink brandy after brandy to steady my nerves. Then we drove back to Galway. The following day, David left Biddy's house and went to live with his new family.

To this day, I don't understand why a child would be given to adoptive parents when the birth mother hadn't made up her mind about what she was doing. I can say with absolute certainty that I never said the words 'I would like to have my child adopted' to anyone. All I expressed was doubt and ambivalence. What if I had said in July or August or any time before I signed the adoption papers that I wanted to keep my baby? And why, months before those papers were signed, should I have lost the right to see my own son? It was very clear that my 'best interests' had been decided, as had those of my baby, and I did not have any meaningful say in it.

16

Back to work

There was no reason to stay in Galway now that I had lost all access to David and my maternity leave was coming to an end so, on 5 July, I left the farmhouse in Ardrahan. I was heartbroken to be saying goodbye to the Cannons. That family had shown me such hospitality and understanding and their home was one of the few places where I had been able to spend time with my son. I cried the whole way back to Dublin.

Catherine Moran met me at Heuston Station. She was shocked when she saw me but hugged me tight and made no comment about how awful I looked. She came with me on the bus to Phibsborough and I cried all the way there too. I was back in Shandon Road. Back in a house I didn't want to be in, with my father, who knew nothing at all about David and what I had been through over the past few months. It was fortunate, I suppose, that my father wasn't a man of many words but, nevertheless, from time to time, he would ask how I had got on in Galway. I had to pretend to be cheerful and talk about how the station was bustling and everyone was so kind and how I couldn't believe there was so little crime in the city. I couldn't cry or mourn or express any of my true feelings. It was imperative, or so I was told, that my father be kept in the dark about the baby I had left behind.

I was due back from maternity leave on 21 July. Two weeks prior to that date I received a call from an Inspector Bernard Haughey, asking me to come into the station. He said he had some things he needed to discuss with me before I came back to work.

I had no idea what the inspector might want to talk about. I knew of Bernard Haughey but we had never spoken before. I had been questioned by some of the other inspectors on a number of occasions during my pregnancy but, now that the baby was born, I didn't see what else there was to discuss on that subject. I supposed it must be customary for an inspector to meet with all banghardaí who were returning from maternity leave, in order to catch up on the events of the previous weeks and discuss any changes to protocol.

I felt nervous walking back into Store Street again.

There couldn't be a guard in the station who wasn't aware of the fact that I had been pregnant and had given birth. I knew, from Catherine Moran, that some of them had been asking her about me and how I was doing and when I was coming back. I wondered whether every one of them was judging me and my behaviour.

As I walked up the stairs to Bernard Haughey's office, I met another garda, Joe Gannon. Joe clapped me on the back and said, 'Welcome back, Majella. Hold your head high. You have nothing to be ashamed of.' I thanked him and gave a little smile. It was such a gracious thing for him to say and it really lifted my spirits in that moment.

The meeting with Bernard Haughey was short and to the point. It was apparent that his aim was not to find out how I was doing but to establish what I was doing with my baby. He asked where the child was now and I told him that David was living with a family in Ennis.

'I see,' he said, and asked what I planned to do with David in the long term.

'I don't know,' I replied. 'I haven't decided yet.'

'But the best thing is adoption,' he declared. 'After all, your father doesn't know about the baby. Where would you keep him?'

'You're probably right,' I said.

The inspector told me that I could leave and that he

would see me again on the 21st.

After I left, Bernard Haughey sent the following statement to Harcourt Square garda station, the headquarters for the Dublin Metropolitan Area.

Re: R/Bangharda Abina M. Moynihan, 00338G, Store Street Station Garda Station, D.M.A.

R/Bangharda Moynihan gave birth to a baby boy on the 30th May, 1984. It is the Bangharda's intention to have the baby adopted but she has not as yet signed the necessary consent forms.

The R/Bangharda has not resumed duty to date, but on the 9th July, 1984, I spoke to her and she informed me that her relationship with Fintan Casey was ended and he has told her that there is no prospect of reconciliation. It is not her intention to seek financial support from Fintan Casey.

Signed: *B. Haughey, Inspector*

*

Coming back to work in Store Street in July 1984 was a very different experience to starting out as a bangharda in September 1983. I was back in my old unit, walking the same beat as though nothing had happened, but I felt like a completely different person. I was no longer the girl who had arrived full of ideals and enthusiasm for her new career. In less than a year, my view of An Garda Síochána had changed completely. That organisation, which I had worshipped for so long, had not only failed to support me during the most difficult time of my life but had repeatedly pushed me to give up my child for adoption. So now my son was living with strangers and I was left with a hurt I was powerless to express. All I could do was attempt to bury those feelings as best I could and try to get on with my work.

In addition to going out on patrol, I began to be assigned to cases of rape, incest and child sexual abuse. It was standard practice to entrust cases of that nature to a bangharda, where possible, as it was felt that victims would be more comfortable in the presence of a woman. Even in the 1980s those crimes were not uncommon, and in addition to the cases that presented at Store Street I was also sent out to smaller police stations in north Dublin when a sex offence was reported and there was no bangharda in the station to respond to it. I would go and meet the victim and accompany him or her to the Sexual Assault Treatment Unit in the Rotunda Hospital. I would be present for the medical examination and afterwards I would bring the swabs to the forensic laboratory in garda headquarters and compile the book of evidence.

Although the work was meaningful, I found those cases very disturbing. The victims were generally young women or children and their distress was unlike anything I had ever experienced. It was my job to bring them through the necessary procedures with as much kindness and compassion as possible. I had to use clear and simple language and, when the victim was a child, I often had to use therapy dolls to ascertain the nature of the abuse that had taken place. It was harrowing, at times, and, as there was no such thing as a counselling service or any other professional support for gardaí in 1984, you had to just get on with it.

When I was working with those vulnerable children or even when I was out on the beat, I couldn't help but think of David. Every infant I saw reminded me of him. In the station, from time to time, other guards would ask, 'Is it true that you had a baby?' and it was a relief to say that yes, I had, and to acknowledge that, even as we spoke, he was out in the world somewhere living his little life. Just to speak about him, for a moment, made the yearning I felt for my son a bit easier to bear.

I was still in touch with Sr. Mary Lillis in Clarecare: I called her every few weeks and left a message, asking about David and how he was doing. When she returned the calls, she'd give only snippets of information about him – he had a hernia; he had had an operation; he loved the company of adults and he was getting on very well with his new family. The reality was, of course, that even if we had been on the phone to each other every day, no conversation or detail could ever have made up for his absence in my life.

It was around that time I began drinking to block out my pain. Two or three times a week, I'd go out with a gang of guards from Store Street – our nights would start in Keating's pub, which was across the road from the station, and then we'd go on to Club Nassau in the Kildare Street Hotel or to the Garda Club or to the Mont Clare Hotel. We'd go out at seven or eight in the evening and I was rarely home before 2 a.m. Other nights, I would stay over with Catherine Moran or visit friends and drink with them in their house. As long as I was in company, drinking, I could escape from my thoughts. It was the only relief possible from the torment of being alone with them; alone without my baby son.

17

The crime of sex and birth

On 23 October 1984 I arrived in work at 5.40 p.m. for the evening shift. After parade I went out on the beat, but shortly after 6.30 p.m. I got a message over the radio: 'Majella, return to the station, please.'

Back in Store Street I was told by Sergeant Pat Dixon, the station house officer, to go upstairs, to an office on the second floor, where there was somebody waiting to speak to me. 'Do you know what this is all about?' I asked him. The sergeant shrugged.

In the office upstairs, a senior guard was sitting behind a desk. He introduced himself as T.P. Corbett and told me he was the investigating officer in a discipline case that was being prepared against me. I had no idea what he was talking about. 'A discipline case, Sir? There must be some mistake. Are you sure I'm the person you're looking for?' 'I know exactly who you are, Recruit Bangharda Moynihan,' he replied. 'Then what did I do?' I asked.

'Did you give birth to a baby in May of this year?' barked the chief superintendent.

'I did,' I replied.

'And was the father of that child also a recruit garda?' he asked.

'He was,' I said.

'It appears therefore that you may have been in breach of discipline,' he said, 'and I am here to take your statement, should you be inclined to give one.'

My legs started to shake. Was this really happening? I wanted to shout, 'What are you doing? I have done nothing wrong!' Afraid my legs would give way, I sat down in the small wooden chair opposite the chief superintendent. He then issued me with the caution that I myself had given many times to those accused of robbery or rape or assault or vandalism: 'You are not obliged to say anything unless you wish to do so, but anything you do say may be taken down in writing and given as evidence.'

I was being treated like a suspected criminal and for what? For giving birth to a baby? For having a relationship with that baby's father? I felt sick to my stomach.

I knew, of course, that I would have to give a statement

– as far as I was concerned, a recruit bangharda refusing anything asked of her by a chief superintendent would have meant the end of her career – and so I told T.P. Corbett I was happy to comply with his request. That was when the interrogation began. I was asked questions that night which no person should have to answer in the whole course of their life. Corbett asked me about my childhood, my relationships, my sexual history: 'Was Fintan Casey the first man you ever had sex with? How long were you together? When did you commence having sexual intercourse? Where did you have sexual intercourse? Did you use condoms? How did you get pregnant? Why didn't you tell your father about the baby?' Things about my life that he had no right to know; things that had nothing to do with the fact that I had been pregnant and had given birth.

When he was finished his questions, the chief superintendent prepared the following statement and requested that I sign it. None of his questions were included in the statement:

Statement of Ban Garda Abina M. Moynihan, Store Street Station, taken at Store Street Station by Chief Superintendent T.P. Corbett on the 23.10.1984.

I am 22 years of age. I joined the Garda Force on the 27th April, 1983. On completion of training I was allocated to Store Street Station on the 30th September, 1983. On this date, 23.10.1984, I was served with a Notice under Regulation 9 of the Garda Síochána (Discipline) Regulations, 1971. I wish to make a statement. Before I joined the Garda Force I was working in Dublin. In the Garda Club, Harrington Street, I met Fintan Casey, [of] Virginia, Co. Cavan and became friendly with him, this was around December, 1982. We were anxious to join the Gardaí. Fintan Casey joined the Force on the 15.12.1982, and I joined in April, 1983. We continued our friendship while in Templemore. Fintan Casey completed his training on the 19.5.1983 and allocated to ███████, Co. Donegal on the 19.5.1983. When Fintan left for ███████ we still continued our friendship. I visited ███████ about four times during the remaining period of my training in Templemore, these were weekends when I would have a weekend pass. I travelled from Templemore to Dublin by train and then from Dublin to Derry by bus. Fintan Casey collected me in Derry and we then travelled to ███████ in Fintan's car. We stayed in Fintan's flat in ███████. We had sexual intercourse a couple of times there in the flat. In the month of November, 1983, or maybe the end of October, I was convinced that I was pregnant. I had my doubts for some time before that. I would say I became pregnant in August, 1983, as the baby, boy, was born on the 31st May, 1984. Sometime in September, 1983, I told Fintan that I thought I was pregnant. He told me he would do everything to help. On the night of my Passing Out (29.9.1983), I again told him, and he said he would help me. About the beginning of November, 1983, Fintan visited my father at 32, Shandon Road, Phibsboro, Dublin. He spoke to my father, I was in the house but not present during the conversation between them. When Fintan came out, he told me that he had asked my father for permission to marry me, I enquired of Fintan why did he ask him and Fintan replied that we would have to get married. He also told me that he had told his mother. Some ten days after, Fintan again visited me in my house in Shandon Road and said to me that he wasn't prepared for marriage and the child. I asked him what was he going to do, was he just going to walk away. Fintan said 'what's the point in getting married. I'm too young to settle down to marriage and a child'. I didn't know what to do. I knew he was going walk away. He then said that his mother had asked him was he the father of the child and he started laughing. I took that to mean that he didn't want responsibility for the child and that he was only covering up for the child. The friendship began to break up after that. I rang Fintan in ████████ some time in December, 1983, and he just didn't want to know me. I rang him again in January, 1984, and he said 'what you do with your life is your business and what I do with mine, is mine'. I then asked him how am I going to face everybody on my own. He never replied. I then asked him was he going to support me and he said you know where I am. I have had no contact with him since. He has never enquired about the baby. For my pregnancy I visited two doctors, Dr. Sullivan in Cavan town and Dr. Joyce, Kinvara, Co. Galway and got Medical Certificates from them and sent them on to my Station in Store Street. The first member I informed of my condition was Inspector ████████ and then my District Officer, Mr. O'Reilly. I also applied to Mr O'Reilly for Maternity Leave and he granted it to me. Sometime before I resumed duty in July, 1984, I informed Inspector Haughey that I had given birth to a baby boy in Galway Regional Hospital on the 31.5.1984. I stayed with a family in the Kinvara area for some time before and after the birth of my baby. The baby was christened David. I now have the baby up for adoption and that should be finalised in the first week of ████████ 1984. I have heard this statement read over to me and it is correct.

SIGNED: *Abina M. Moynihan, 00338G, R/BGarda*

WITNESS: *Thomas P. Corbett, Chief Superintendent*

DATE: *23rd October, 1984*

Corbett told me that my statement would be sent to garda headquarters and that in due course I would be informed about the next steps in the case. Then he walked out of the office with my statement tucked under his arm. I put my head in my hands and cried.

I stayed in the office for twenty minutes and then washed my face in the ladies' bathroom, went downstairs and walked out on the beat. I remember wandering around Beresford Place in a daze. I didn't want to tell anyone what had happened – that would only compound my shame – so I spent the night avoiding other guards and stayed away from the station on my breaks. When my shift was finished, I hurried home and went straight to bed.

The chief superintendent hadn't told me anything about the disciplinary process, beyond the fact that I would have to wait to hear back from garda headquarters. After a few days, the events of 23 October began to seem like a bad dream and I started to hope that maybe that would be the end of the matter. But on 1 November I arrived at work and was informed there was a Superintendent James Harahan to see me. I was shown to a small room off the kitchen.

Harahan was tall and his expression was cold and disapproving. He introduced himself, then asked, 'Are you Bangharda Abina Moynihan?' 'I am, Sir,' I said, 'though I don't go by that name. I go by the name Majella.' 'Well, Majella,' he said, 'you are being disciplined.' He commenced reading out the charges against me, which were as follows:

CONDUCT PREJUDICIAL TO DISCIPLINE OR LIKELY TO BRING DISCREDIT ON THE FORCE, that is to say, that between the 20th May, 1983 and about the 30th September, 1983, you, being an unmarried female member of An Garda Síochána, did associate on terms of intimacy and undue familiarity with, one, Recruit Garda Fintan Casey, Registered Number: 23127D, an unmarried male member of An Garda Síochána stationed at ███████ Garda Station, ███████, Co. Donegal and during such period of association you had sexual intercourse with said Recruit Garda Fintan Casey in the County Donegal Area as a result of which you became pregnant and gave birth to a male child at Galway Regional Hospital, Galway, County

Galway on or about the 31st May, 1984.
The said Conduct Prejudicial to Discipline or
Likely to Bring Discredit on the Force is a breach
of Discipline within the meaning of Regulation 6
of the Garda Síochána (Discipline) Regulations,
1971 and is described at Reference Number 1 in
the Schedule to the said Regulations.

After he read out the first charge, I stopped him and
said, 'I don't understand, Sir. Why are you charging me?
I haven't committed a criminal offence.' 'You are in
breach of the Garda Síochána Discipline Regulations,'
he said, and then continued on to read the second charge.

CONDUCT PREJUDICIAL TO DISCIPLINE
OR LIKELY TO BRING DISCREDIT ON
THE FORCE, that is to say, that you being
a female member of An Garda Síochána
stationed at Store Street Garda Station, Dublin,
did on or about the 31st May, 1984 give
birth to a child outside wedlock at Galway
Regional Hospital, Galway, County Galway.
The said Conduct Prejudicial to Discipline or
Likely to Bring Discredit on the Force is a breach
of Discipline within the meaning of Regulation 6
of the Garda Síochána (Discipline) Regulations,
1971 and is described at Reference Number 1 in
the Schedule to the said Regulations.

After he read out the second charge, he said, just as T.P. Corbett had done, 'You are not obliged to say anything unless you wish to do so, but anything you do say may be taken down in writing and given as evidence.'

'Superintendent,' I sobbed, 'could I lose my job?'

'That, Bangharda Moynihan, will be subject to adjudication,' he replied. 'You may be cautioned, you may be reprimanded, you may be fined or you may be dismissed.' Then he added, somewhat sardonically: 'You cannot be reduced in rank, as you are already at the lowest rank.' 'How will I know which it is, Sir?' I asked. 'You will be summoned either to a sworn or an unsworn enquiry, at a date yet to be decided. The former is a formal hearing, presided over by a chief superintendent, with evidence required and witnesses called. The second is a less formal hearing and may involve only yourself and a presiding officer.'

Harahan, his task now completed, gathered his things and prepared to leave. He paused, looked across at me and said, 'If you had gone to England and had an abortion, you would not have brought discredit on the garda force.' Then he walked out of the room.

All these years later it's hard to imagine a senior officer in An Garda Síochána telling a subordinate she should have terminated her pregnancy and that by failing to do so she had brought shame on the guards. I still recall the shock I felt upon hearing those words. That a man like Superintendent Harahan, for whom

I would have had the utmost respect, would feel it was appropriate to tell me I ought to have had an abortion. That a man so wholly unconnected to me would feel it proper that he should sit in judgement of my most intimate acts. As a trainee bangharda, I went to Templemore and took an oath to protect life and property. And yet when I tried to do just that I was told I had disgraced myself and my colleagues.

Until that moment, I hadn't understood what was motivating the guards to investigate my private life. After all, Fintan and I were consenting adults and we hadn't broken any laws. We weren't the first gardaí to have sex outside of wedlock and we certainly wouldn't be the last. But it was clear now that the problem was not so much that I had become pregnant but that I had remained pregnant. Instead of taking steps to hide my situation, I had made it apparent for all to see, and in the process I had become a nuisance, an embarrassment and, worst of all, a bad example to other banghardaí. The question, as far as senior gardaí were concerned, was not whether I should be punished but how.

I don't know how I managed to walk out of the station that night and go back on patrol. I can still feel the desperation I felt as I walked up Talbot Street. When I got to North Earl Street, I bought a packet of cigarettes in a newsagent's, then went into Burger King and got a coffee. I knew the manager in there a little and she came over when she saw I was crying and asked what was wrong. I told her it was nothing. I didn't want to confide in anyone. There was no one I felt I could trust.

My mind was racing. Over and over, I repeated the charges to myself as though to confirm that this was really happening; that I was under investigation for having had sexual intercourse and, then, for having given birth to a child. My son, who was not even six months old, was regarded as a discredit to the force and my sexual behaviour was being discussed throughout the organisation – all the way up to garda headquarters. It was more than I could bear

That night, in the bathroom in Shandon Road, marked the first time in my life that I harmed myself. It was a cry for help – a razor cut to my wrists the only way I could think of to ease the pain. I was losing my child and now it looked likely that I was going to lose my job too. I couldn't see any future for myself that wasn't full of misery and shame. Thankfully, it was a superficial injury not requiring any medical intervention, but the pain I was in was deep, searing, and bound, in time, to take its course.

18

The bishop and the bangharda

After the events of that terrible night, I knew I had to tell someone what was happening. If I didn't establish some kind of support system, it wouldn't be long before my circumstances would once again seem too much to bear. I was scared to think of what I might do the next time.

I decided to go to Mena Robinson in CURA. She, at least, knew all about my pregnancy and was neither a member of An Garda Síochána nor a family member, and at that time I believed her to be a straightforward ally.

I would later realise that my relationship with Mena was far more complex than I, at twenty-two years old, could have understood. As a counsellor for

CURA, a crisis pregnancy agency affiliated with the Catholic Church, Mena was part of a system that was separating Irish women from their babies. Although I found her support invaluable at the time, Mena was one of many people in my life whom I believe were less interested in presenting me with options than they were in encouraging me to give my baby to what Mena herself described as 'a good, decent family'.

Mena did feel she had my best interests at heart – that by facilitating my son's adoption, she was assisting me in a time of need and providing a better outcome for David than he was likely to have with his own, single mother. But adoption was not the right thing, not for me nor, I believed, for my baby. Nowadays, Irish society is more compassionate to single mothers. We have moved on from the ethos of CURA and no longer think it desirable that unmarried mothers would be separated from their babies. I wasn't at all surprised when the agency was wound up in 2018, citing a lack of demand for its services.

A few days after the charges were preferred against me, I visited Mena in her office in CURA on Marlborough Street. Whenever I dropped in to see her, Mena would always say, 'Ah! Hello, Majella!' and make me a cup of coffee. When I told her what had happened, she was appalled. 'They cannot do this to you,' she said. 'Well, they have,' I replied.

Mena was a smoker. She lit a cigarette and said, 'I just can't believe it. This is the 80s.'

I began to see Mena once or twice a week. I would call in to her when I was out on the beat or during my lunch break. I always found her to be a comforting presence. I still hadn't made any definitive decision about David and, by then, it was only a matter of weeks until I would have to sign the adoption papers, so I spent hours with Mena in her office, agonising about what to do. Her advice was always the same: 'Give him to a family who can take care of him.'

I also kept Mena informed about the goings-on at work, where it was clear that the internal garda investigation against me had intensified. Almost every day I was being held back after parade and questioned by the Store Street inspectors for an hour or more. I didn't know it then but the investigating officer in my case, Chief Superintendent T.P. Corbett, had also been gathering statements about me from my colleagues and superiors. These statements were not made available to me at the time but were kept in my garda file and I read them many years later.

Statement of Inspector ▮▮▮▮▮

In January 1984, as a result of a telephone call from Mrs. Robinson, 'Cura', I went to her office in Marlboro Street, where I met B/Garda Majella Moynihan, Store Street. She informed me that she was three months pregnant. She was very upset and depressed and stated that her one and only ambition was to become a B/Garda and now she had let down the whole force and felt utterly ashamed. She informed me that the father of the child she was expecting was a member of the Garda with whom she had been keeping company at one time and had renewed acquaintances while both were on their Part I Training Course at Templemore. I now know this member to be R/Garda Fintan Casey, stationed at ███████ Co. Donegal. B/Garda Moynihan informed me that when she discovered she was pregnant she told Fintan Casey of her condition on the day of her passing out. She said that they also told his mother of her condition, who promised her every support. She informed me that at Christmas 1983, Fintan Casey asked her father for his consent to their marriage, to which he agreed. Her father was never aware of her pregnancy. I spoke to her Step-Mother on several occasions and she informed me that her father could not be told. It appears from Christmas on, Majella did not see Fintan and any telephone communication with him was evasive. She was beginning to feel that she was not going to hear from him anymore but did not know where she stood. She was deeply hurt as she felt there was a great relationship between them. She informed me that she was advised to go for an abortion which suggestion was repugnant to her. I informed her then that the District Officer would have to be informed. She stated that she was about to tell him a few days earlier but lost her courage. I arranged to accompany her to the District Officer but eventually she herself informed him. As a result she was gainfully employed on indoor duties until she went on maternity leave. Mrs. Robinson, 'Cura', arranged that she stay at an address in Galway during her final weeks of pregnancy. On the 31st May 1984, she gave birth to a baby boy at the Regional Hospital, Galway and whom she named David. The baby is now with his adoptive parents. I kept in contact with B/Garda Moynihan all through her pregnancy. She had a difficult time, was depressed at times and found it hard to come to terms with the fact that someone she trusted so much had let her down and whom she felt could have given her at least moral support at that time. She was at all times anxious and concerned about the baby and subsequent welfare and made up her mind to do what was best for her child. Finally, she made the ultimate sacrifice in placing her child for adoption where he would have the benefit of a good family home and upbringing. B/Garda Moynihan is the victim of circumstances having been placed in an orphanage herself at 3 years of age due to the death of her Mother and remained there until her secondary education was completed. She has no grievance whatever about being institutionalised but it is my opinion that such conditions left its mark which was apparent during her training at Templemore. I firmly believe that B/Garda Moynihan yearned for love, affection and companionship which she thought she had found in her association with Fintan Casey. I believe she has reached full maturity through the hard road of experience and I believe she will make a successful career in the Garda Síochána.

Signed: ███████, *B/Inspector*

Statement of Inspector Michael J. Francis

I have found the member to be honest, dependable and willing to learn her job. She has the correct attitude towards her superiors.

I have discussed policing and police duties with her and given her guidance in the matter of proofs in court and accident investigation procedure. I have noticed in particular about this member that she listens attentively and has a very strong will to succeed as a Ban Garda. It is my opinion that she will make an efficient member of the force.

Signed: *Michael J. Francis, Inspector*

Statement of Superintendent G.B. Curran
Re: R/Bangharda Abina M. Moynihan, 00338G,
Store Street Station, D.M.A.

I am satisfied that she is doing her work satisfactorily and I have no complaints about her.

Having spoken to the young lady and in view of the circumstances of this incident I consider her suitable for retention in the Force. Her child has been adopted and she is now dedicated to her job. I would not recommend disciplinary action.

Signed: *G.B. Curran, Superintendent*

Statement of Chief Superintendent T.J. O'Reilly
Re: R/Bangharda Abina M. Moynihan, 00338G,
Store Street Station.

I have spoken with R/Bangharda Moynihan on a number of occasions. I am satisfied that she is suitable for retention in the Force.

I have given all aspects of this matter careful consideration. I do not consider Disciplinary action appropriate in this case and I do not recommend same.

Signed: *T.J. O'Reilly, Chief Superintendent*

Statement of Assistant Commissioner John Fleming

I am satisfied B/Garda Moynihan is suitable for retention in the Force. I do not recommend disciplinary action.

Signed: *John Fleming, Assistant Commissioner, 'B' Branch*

Chief Superintendent Corbett also took a statement from Gerry Corcoran, a recruit garda who had been stationed in Donegal and living in digs with Fintan in the summer of 1983, while I was in Templemore and occasionally visiting.

Statement of R/Garda Gerard Corcoran, 23158D, Bridewell Garda Station, made to Chief Superintendent T.P. Corbett, at the Bridewell Station, on the 25.10.1984.

I joined the Garda Síochána on the 15.12.1982, on completion of training at Templemore Training Centre on 19.5.1983, I was allocated to ████████, Co. Donegal on the 20.5.1983. I know R/Garda Fintan Casey, he was also in Templemore with me, but in a different class. He was also allocated to ████████ on the same date as me. In ████████ we were both in the same digs in Mrs. Grayson, ███████ ████████, about 3 to 4 miles from the station. We were sleeping in the same room. I also know R/Ban Garda Majella Moynihan. She came to Templemore some months after us. Majella Moynihan and Fintan Casey were friendly with each other while in Templemore, they went around together. They appeared to have known each other before they joined the Force. After Fintan Casey and I were transferred to ██████████ Majella Moynihan visited Fintan Casey there on a couple of weekends and stayed in Mrs. Grayson's house but in a different room to us. She could have visited ████████ on other occasions when I would be away on my long week-ends, I believe she did on one occasion as far as I know. I don't think they were engaged. I know that on one occasion after Majella Moynihan passed out from Templemore and transferred to Store Street, she visited Fintan Casey in ██████████ and I was talking to her. She was talking about her job in Dublin. She could have visited ████████ on other occasions, I am not sure. I was transferred to the Bridewell on the 17.1.1984. For a good while before Christmas 1983, say a month or two, I know that the relationship then had ceased, Fintan Casey himself told me. He gave me no reason. Before I left ███████████ I heard a rumour that Majella Moynihan was pregnant, I don't know where that rumour originated. Some time after I came to the Bridewell I heard she was pregnant, because of the rumours going around. I have heard this statement read over to me. It is correct.

Signed: *Gerry Corcoran, Garda, 23158D*

Witness: *Thomas P. Corbett, Chief Superintendent*

Date: *25th October, 1984*

A statement was even taken from Mrs. Grayson, Fintan's landlady.

Statement of Mrs. Grayson, ████████ ████████ ████████, Co. Donegal

I reside at above address. Garda Fintan Casey, ████████ Station has been lodging with me since May, 1983. Garda Smith was here about three or four weeks when he asked me if I knew any boarding house where his friend Majella could stay. I told him that I would keep her. Towards the end of June, 1983, Majella came on a Friday and left on a Monday. She occupied a room alone while staying. About August, 1983, she returned and stayed for a weekend only and occupied a room on her own on the occasion. I have not seen her since then.

Signed: *Elma Grayson*
Witness: *J.J. O'Neill, Superintendent*
Date: *24/10/84*

It is my belief that the purpose of these statements was to build the case against me in order that the garda commissioner, Larry Wren, could determine how I was to be disciplined. To this day, I find it heartening that my senior officers were complimentary about me and my work and did not feel that disciplinary action would be appropriate in my case.

Their recommendations appeared to have little impact on the commissioner's thinking. Two weeks after the charges were preferred against me, on an evening in mid-November, the female inspector asked me to stay back after parade to speak to her. In her office, she asked me to sit down and then she said, 'Majella, the talk among senior guards is that you're going to be let go. You're going to lose your job.'

Although I was aware that the commissioner had the right, under the Garda Discipline Regulations, to dismiss me from the force if he felt my behaviour had rendered me unfit to serve, and Superintendent Harahan had informed me that this was a possibility, it was not the outcome I had been expecting. I was shocked and devastated. She told me that, had I not been on probation, the commissioner would have required the consent of the minister for justice to sack me, but as it was, he could do so at his own discretion, and this being the case, I should prepare myself for the worst.

As soon as the meeting ended, I went straight to Mena and told her about the rumour. Mena, who was a small, bespectacled and generally unassuming woman, could nevertheless be firm when she wanted to be. When she heard that I was going to be sacked, she said, 'Oh no you won't be, Majella. Oh no you won't.'

Mena said she would consult Father Pat O'Donoghue, a priest in the Pro Cathedral who also worked with the Rotunda Girls Aid Society, the adoption society that Mena worked for. Her plan was that she and Father O'Donoghue would contact the archbishop of Dublin, Kevin McNamara, and ask him to speak to the garda commissioner on my behalf.

The following day Mena called me in Shandon Road and told me her plan had been successful: a meeting had been arranged between the archbishop and the garda commissioner and she and Father Pat O'Donoghue would also be in attendance. She promised to let me know the outcome of the meeting as soon as she possibly could.

The day after the meeting I met Mena in her office. 'It's good news,' she said, 'but only because the archbishop intervened. Otherwise you would have been out on your ear.' Mena told me that she and Father Pat had sat in on the entire meeting and that Commissioner Larry Wren had confirmed to Archbishop McNamara that his intention was to dismiss me from the force. The archbishop objected, on the grounds that if this was the treatment meted out to me it would be a lesson to other banghardaí who became pregnant out of wedlock that they had better have an abortion. 'If you sack Majella,' he said, 'you'll open the gates for England.' It was decided there and then, between those two powerful men, that I was to be cautioned. And so it was that the archbishop of Dublin saved my job.

When I heard I wasn't going to be sacked, something like delight flooded through me. Even after all that had happened to me, some part of me still felt that this was the job of my dreams. It makes me sad to think of it now, given what would unfold.

19

David's adoption

5th November, 1984

Dear Majella,
It's high time you heard from me. Thanks for
your letter at the beginning of September.
I went to see David three weeks ago. He is the
image of you – at least I think so. Desmond and
Maeve are really proud of him and love showing
him off. He is getting very big now. His hair is
light brown in colour. He takes five bottles every
day. Also he takes rice, an egg sometimes and
rusks. He is teething at the moment, but he is a
really good baby, and they love him very much.

I'm sorry it has taken me so long to answer your letter – I won't be as bad the next time.
Best wishes, Majella.
Your sincerely,
Mary Lillis (Sr.)
Social Worker

December, 1984

Sr. M. Lillis,
Thanks for your letter. I was glad to hear that David is getting on fine. I am still so mixed up. I hope God encourages me to do the right thing.
Love,
Majella (M.)

By the winter of 1984, Sr. Mary Lillis and I were no longer communicating by phone about David and were merely exchanging letters. Sometimes it was months before I got a reply.

By December, the option to keep David was still legally open to me but the time to make a decision was fast approaching. Given my state of mind, I was in no position to be making a decision about the long-term welfare of my child. I was still awaiting the conclusion of the garda disciplinary investigation into my pregnancy and that process had destroyed what was left of my self-esteem. I thought of myself as dirty, promiscuous and – that terrible word – a 'slut'. Who was I to try to raise a little boy, teach him right from wrong and set him a good example? How could a girl like me provide a suitable environment for a child to grow up in?

If I had been supported by An Garda Síochána, I have no doubt that I would have kept my son. It would have been difficult raising him alone but I had a perfectly good salary – almost £7,000 per annum, with increases year on year, which wasn't bad in 1984 – and, as long as I knew I wasn't going to lose it, my situation would not have seemed hopeless. Instead, I had been put through the wringer. I had been charged with breaching discipline, accused of bringing discredit on the force, questioned about my sexual conduct and threatened with dismissal. By December 1984, I had reached a point where I would have done just about anything the guards asked me to do to keep my job and salvage what was left of my reputation.

Nobody had ever so much as broached with me the practical or psychological consequences of giving up my son. I did not know that there would be no support for me once my baby was gone, that I wouldn't have the right to send him a letter or a card or a birthday present. I did not know that I would feel guilt and remorse for the rest of my life, or that I would never stop thinking about him, even for a second.

In the end, the decision to have my child adopted was made by so many people. By my stepmother, who urged me to hide my pregnancy and keep my baby a secret; by Fintan, who walked out on me and on his unborn son, when we needed him to stand by us; by CURA and Clarecare, who told me time and time again that my child would be better off with a respectable family; and, above all, by An Garda Síochána, who, from the moment I told them I was pregnant, interrogated, shamed and hounded me, and insisted that adoption was the only appropriate course of action. I was forced into making that decision because, as I saw it, I wasn't strong enough to stand up to them all and for that I was full of recrimination and self-blame. To this day, I find it hard to forgive myself, and yet I know that, in reality, I didn't stand a chance. After all, while I might legally have had a choice, there was no meaningful choice open to me. To go it alone would have been to become an outcast.

On 5 December I took a bus to Clare to sign what was described as the Final Consent. In Ennis courthouse I sat on a bench as the clerk read out the adoption papers, then gave them to me to sign. It was totally impersonal. I hardly knew what I was signing. I certainly didn't understand the damage I was about to do to myself. I didn't realise that the impact of that moment would reverberate through the rest of my life. This was my child. He was a human being and he was mine and all they wanted was my signature so they could take him away.

It is the great regret of my life that I signed the papers that day.

32, Shandon Road,
Phibsboro,
Dublin 7.
12/01/85

Dear Sr. M. Lillis,
I hope you are well settled after Christmas and New Year.

Sr, I am writing to ask you could you get photos of David from six months to now because I want to have them to be able to look back at and realise what I have done is for the better, because there is so many times I have questioned my mind and am not able to come up with a sensible conclusion why this whole thing had to take place. I am just worried about David. I know I shouldn't be because Maeve and Desmond are so nice and loving.

Could you forward the photos as soon as you can.

Thanking you for everything.
Good luck in '85.
Take care,
Majella

22nd February, 1985

Dear Majella,
Thanks for your letter which I got last month. I'm enclosing two photographs of David and I hope you like them. He's just himself in them so that's why I enclose these two. He's in great form, as good as gold and has been fine since the surgery. I was sorry to hear you have been through such a bad time. I rang home but you had gone away for the weekend.
  I'll finish now, Majella.
  God Bless,
  Mary (Lillis)
  Social Worker

The records in Clarecare describe the reason for David's adoption as follows:

David's natural parents knew each other for about 2½ years when she became pregnant. At first they planned to get married but then decided against it because he felt he may not be able to cope with the responsibility of having a child. She was very hurt about this in the beginning but has now come to terms with it. She decided on Adoption because she wanted David to have two parents to love and to care for him, and she felt she could not provide this security herself.

She is very happy about David and feels that she has done the right thing in placing him for Adoption.

20

Hitting the headlines

On 5 February 1985 I was called to Harcourt Square, the garda headquarters of the Dublin Metropolitan Region, to hear the conclusion of my disciplinary case. I knew from Mena Robinson that the outcome was likely to be a caution but I was still nervous. At Harcourt Square I was sent to the office of Chief Superintendent Jim Sullivan. I remember walking into the room and seeing him sitting behind his desk. He didn't stand up or say hello, but looked me up and down and simply said, 'If it happens you again, Bangharda Moynihan, you're sacked.' He told me then that I could leave. That was my caution.

Though the meeting with the chief superintendent had felt like a slap in the face, as I left his office that day

I thought, Well, at least that's an end to it. I hoped that somehow I could start again in An Garda Síochána. It was less than two years since I had been called to Templemore, I was still at the very start of my career and yet it felt as though I had done enough damage to end ten garda careers.

The following day I went into work for 9.30 a.m. On the way in I met Catherine Moran. We were generally delighted to see each other but that morning, she seemed nervous about something. In the station, it seemed as though everyone had suddenly stopped talking the moment I walked in. An inspector, Tom Connolly, approached me and said, 'Majella, I need to see you in my office.'

I felt a rush of panic and asked, 'Please, Sir, can Catherine come with me?' The inspector nodded and led us up the stairs in silence.

In Tom Connolly's office the desk was covered in newspapers. 'You're front-page news,' he said. I looked at his splayed copy of the *Irish Times* and saw that under the lead story, which was about the Kerry Babies case, there was an article that was obviously about me. The headline was 'Garda discipline move on birth' and the piece, by the journalist Mary Maher, described 'an unmarried ban-gharda who had a baby last year' who was now 'awaiting the outcome of disciplinary proceedings taken against her under Garda Síochána regulations'. It detailed the precise charges that I faced: that I had 'consorted' with an unnamed garda and given birth to a baby and it included a quote from the general secretary of the Garda Representative Association (GRA), Jack Marrinan:

> We certainly would not encourage our female members to think that this is a normal condition for them to get into, out of wedlock. We would expect our banghardaí to be moral in every way and we would not think that their morals are always or necessarily their own private business.

The report also referred to a number of other female members of the force who had become pregnant and the response of An Garda Síochána in each case. It seemed that at least one of the women had been treated with more compassion and care than I had:

> One woman was transferred following the birth of her baby to a location near her home, where arrangements were made to care for the baby while she continued working. In another one, a pregnant ban-gharda was instructed by her superior to marry the father of her child, but succeeded in resisting the instruction and retained her post.

The story was covered in several other papers and in a

level of detail that could only mean it had been given to the press by a member of An Garda Síochána. The papers had copies of the charge sheets, which must have come from my file, and most of the articles referred to the fact that I was serving in a garda station in Dublin city centre. I felt horribly betrayed, collapsing to the ground in despair. 'What else are ye going to do to me?' I sobbed. Tom Connolly didn't respond. He just left me to cry and then told Catherine and me that we could have the rest of the day off. Outside the station, I told Catherine that I wanted to die. And I really did. I felt, then, that there was no limit to what the guards were willing to put me through. It hurt to know that a colleague had passed on the most personal and private details about me to the papers. It hurt to think that my whole life was out there in the media and everyone I knew was reading about it and talking about it.

I decided to go to Mena Robinson. Catherine insisted on coming with me. As we walked down O'Connell Street she pointed to a newsstand, where a sign on a sandwich board read 'Bangharda may be dismissed for having a baby'. 'I saw it on my way in, Majella,' she said. 'I knew that it was you.' We looked at each other in silence for a moment and Catherine squeezed my hand. 'It's not fair, Majella,' she said. 'You don't deserve any of this.'

We stayed with Mena for hours. When I told her what had happened, she called Store Street and inquired as to who had given my file to a journalist. She was put through to an inspector, who said, 'No one in this station would have sold that story to a newspaper. No doubt it was Majella herself who spoke to a journalist.' I was furious. The idea that I would have wanted to publicise the details of my disgrace was ludicrous. To this day I cannot believe he had the nerve to suggest it.

That evening I went back to Shandon Road. After dinner my father and Kitty and I sat down together in the living room to watch the six o'clock news. When the newsreader, Don Cockburn, mentioned 'an unmarried bangharda facing disciplinary action for having a baby', I felt the blood drain from my face. Kitty turned to me with a look of concern. As soon as she saw my expression she realised I was the bangharda in question. Neither of us said a word. The silence was eventually broken by my father, who hadn't noticed anything out of the ordinary in my behaviour or Kitty's. 'Do you know that girl?' he asked. 'No,' I replied.

The papers continued to run the story the following day. Whoever had leaked the details of my case must have told them the outcome because all the headlines stated that I had been cautioned. Mary Maher in the *Irish Times* described this as 'the mildest form of sanction' and added that it would not appear on my record. She said it was understood that the decision had been reached by the garda commissioner, Larry Wren, and that 'the case of the male garda, who is the acknowledged father of the child' was with the Department of Justice. She also noted that as the father of the child had finished his period of probation and was a fully attested member of the force, 'he would now be able to contest any decision to dismiss him before a full sworn enquiry'.

Following the media coverage of my case the subject was raised in the Dáil, when Proinsias De Rossa and the late David Molony questioned then Minister for Justice Michael Noonan about his role in my proceedings and why he hadn't intervened. The minister told both TDs that under garda regulations the enforcement of discipline within the force was a matter for the garda authorities. 'I have no function in the matter,' he said. 'Accordingly, it would not be appropriate for me to comment either on the specific case referred to or on the other issues raised.'

Later, in 2009, he would respond in a similar way when I called his office and put those same questions to him myself.

21

Cross-examined

Although my relationship with Fintan had ended with that telephone conversation in January 1984, I was still surprised that he had never once contacted me after David was born. I thought he might have cared to know if our child was a boy or a girl. I thought he might have wondered about my plans for the baby's future. I thought, at the very least, he might have wanted a photograph or a keepsake of his son. By the spring of 1985, it had been more than fifteen months since I had heard from him. When I thought of him at all, it was with bitterness and resentment. I hoped I would never see him again.

In the third week of April, the female inspector told me that Fintan's sworn inquiry was to be held at the end of the month and I would be expected to attend. 'You can have a lift up with me,' she added, 'because I also have to give a statement to the inquiry.'

'Oh?' I replied.

'Yes', she said, 'I'll be asked what I knew about your pregnancy and how I supported you at the time.'

I was stunned. 'Okay,' I said, 'I'll take the lift' and left the room.

The very last thing I wanted to do was stand in a room with the man who had abandoned me and our baby and submit to questioning about our sexual history. But that, it seemed, was what was being demanded of me. And how could I object? The inquiry was taking place at the behest of the garda commissioner; my superior officers in Store Street would be attending to testify about me; and as for the Garda Representative Association (GRA), whose stated mission was to defend their members and promote their interests, its general secretary Jack Marrinan had already declared on the record that:

> The Association wouldn't like it to go out – I wouldn't like it to go out because I am the father of a young lady myself – I wouldn't like anybody to think that [a bangharda becoming pregnant out of wedlock] would be regarded as the normal condition or appropriate behaviour.

I was hardly going to turn to the GRA for help.

The sworn inquiry was scheduled for 30 April. On the afternoon of the 29th, the inspector came to Shandon Road to collect me. I took an overnight bag and told Kitty and my father that I was working a late shift. The inspector stood in the hall and said nothing. In the car, she introduced me to her husband, a superintendent. I had never met him before, though I knew him by reputation. It was intimidating to meet any senior garda under those circumstances and neither he nor his wife made much of an effort to set me at ease. There was little or no conversation as we travelled up to Donegal and I got the impression that the superintendent resented both the trip and the miscreant recruit who had made it a necessity. I felt like a naughty child being brought to her punishment.

The inspector had arranged that the three of us would stay the night at the Mount Errigal Hotel in Letterkenny. Her husband suggested we have dinner in the hotel restaurant. I went along, but after moving my food around long enough for it to seem as if I had eaten something, I excused myself and went to my room.

In the bathroom, I splashed water on my face and noticed my hands were shaking. There were mere hours now before I would have to appear at the inquiry. I'd had no preparation for cross-examination and no one had told me what questions to expect but

I assumed the interrogation would be pointed and personal. I lay on the bed and tried to sleep.

I awoke the next morning full of dread. There was no question of eating breakfast, so I put on my uniform and sat in my room until it was time to go and meet the inspector and her husband in the lobby. It was a short drive from the hotel to Letterkenny garda station and by the time we arrived, my insides felt leaden and it was an effort to walk. I skulked behind the inspector as she introduced herself to the station guards and told them we were there for the sworn inquiry. We were sent to a waiting room on the first floor and the guards sought, with little regard for subtlety, to catch a glimpse of the pale, disgraced bangharda who was making her way upstairs.

The sworn inquiry was being held in the main office in the garda station and the inspector paused outside the door to try to hear whether the proceedings had begun. 'I'm sure you won't have long to wait,' she said as we sat down. I fidgeted nervously with my skirt and tried not to think about what was about to happen. After all, there was nothing I could do to prevent it. If I wanted to keep my job, this was another hoop through which I would have to jump for An Garda Síochána.

A few minutes later, a sergeant with a Donegal accent came into the waiting room and said, 'We're ready for you now.' He led me across the hall to an office, which had been set up to look like a courtroom.

At the head of the room three men sat at a top table, as though they were presiding at a tribunal. All three were dressed in the trappings of their rank – a chief superintendent and two superintendents.

The sergeant who had led me into the office took a seat at a small desk beside a stenographer, who was the only other woman in the room. At a table on the right sat Fintan Casey and another man with whom Fintan was conferring.

In the centre of the room, between all three tables, there was an empty chair. It was in this chair that I was directed to sit by the chief superintendent, who then proceeded to take a statement from me. I was asked my name, my age, my employment history, the details of my relationship with Fintan and the dates and locations of when he and I had had sexual intercourse. The chief superintendent then sought to establish the approximate timing of my becoming pregnant, the date and location of my giving birth to my son and, finally, whether Fintan Casey was the only man with whom I had ever had sexual intercourse.

As soon as I sat down, the man next to Fintan stood up and introduced himself. His name, he said, was Garda Lawless, he was Fintan's GRA representative and he would be cross-examining my statement.

I wondered why *I* didn't have anyone to speak on my behalf. There I was, alone in front of all those men, any one of whom could ask anything they liked about my private life and I had to answer promptly and politely, while Fintan never said a word. He sat, tucked away at the side of the room, well defended by his representative.

While I had been charged with two offences – having sex outside marriage and giving birth to a child – Fintan was facing one single charge: that he, being unmarried, did associate on terms of intimacy and undue familiarity and had sexual intercourse with an unmarried female recruit, as a result of which, the said female recruit became pregnant and gave birth to a baby. His representative seemed intent on proving that, if indeed Fintan *had* had sexual intercourse with me, he was only one of many men to have done so, and may not, therefore, have been responsible for the aforementioned pregnancy and childbirth. After some initial questions about my disciplinary case, Garda Lawless went on to ask about my time in Templemore:

Question:- Did you like the atmosphere in the Training Centre?

Answer:- Yes.

Question:- You had opportunities to socialise down there?

Answer:- Yes.

Question:- You socialised throughout your
training period down there?

Answer:- Yes.

Question:- How did you socialise?

Answer:- I went to the pub. All you can do down
there is go to the pub.

Question:- Where was Fintan Casey's passing out
party held?

Answer:- In the Templemore Arms Hotel.

Question:- Did you attend any other passing out
parades, between Fintan's and your own?

Answer:- I didn't get any invitations, but we went
down to the hotel after.

Satisfied that he had demonstrated that I was the kind
of woman who frequented public houses and hotels,
Garda Lawless moved on to questions about my sexual
history. When he and I were together, Fintan had asked
whether he was the first person I had ever been with.
I had told him, then, about Shane O'Connor. This
information had clearly been relayed to Fintan's GRA
representative.

Question:- Have you any difficulty in making
friends socially?

Answer:- No.

Question:- Had you a relationship with anybody before you met Fintan?

Answer:- Yes.

Question:- In your relationship with the person in 1980 and with Fintan in 1982, how did you avoid becoming pregnant?

I was about to answer, when I was interrupted by some harrumphing from the top table. The chief superintendent objected to the question and it was disallowed. Unperturbed, Fintan's representative ventured on to his next tack, which was to sow doubt about the date I had become pregnant.

Question:- Are you quite sure that it was in Shandon Road, Phibsboro that you became pregnant?

Answer:- Yes.

Question:- Did Fintan Casey actually stay there in your house?

Answer:- Yes.

Question:- Do you know the dates?

Answer:- I would say it was the 24th or 25th August, 1983.

Question:- Why are you so sure it was that
particular time you became pregnant?

Answer:- Because three to four weeks after that, I
realised there was something wrong with me,
and suspected pregnancy.

Question:- Did you seek medical advice at that
stage?

Answer:- No.

Question:- Was it in January 1984 you went to
Cura?

Answer:- Yes.

Question:- As a result of going there you got in
contact with B/Inspector ▮▮▮▮▮▮?

Answer:- Yes.

Question:- Did you inform B/Inspector
▮▮▮▮▮▮ at that stage that you were three
months pregnant?

Answer:- If I did it was a mistake, because I was
more than three months. I was four months
and a week pregnant at that time.

Question:- Were you confused about dates at that
time?

Answer:- Yes.

Question:- Would I be correct in saying that you do not pay much attention to dates?

Answer:- At that stage I knew I was on my own, I was confused about everything.

Question:- Had Fintan abandoned you at that stage?

Answer:- Yes. I think it was the 4th January I rang him at ████████.

Question:- How were you confused?

Answer:- I was confused, I was left on my own, I had to face everybody.

It was torture to discuss my most intimate experiences with a room full of men. I was laying bare the feelings I'd had during the worst time of my life and to do so was painful and mortifying. If my testimony had any effect on Fintan, however, I couldn't see it. As I described the suffering caused by his abandonment of me and our baby, his face was entirely blank. His representative must have been aware that this line of questioning was likely to elicit some sympathy for me, if not from Fintan then certainly from the top table, so he changed his approach.

Question:- You told your sister when you thought you were in difficulties first. Did you tell your father?

Answer:- No. I received a phonecall from Mrs. Casey at Store Street and one of the members took a number for me to ring back. I rang the number concerned. Mrs Casey told me that I had to tell my father. I replied 'Why?' and she said, 'He is entitled to know.'

Question:- What was your reaction to that?

Answer:- I said, 'Fair enough, I'll tell him.'

Question:- And did you?

Answer:- No.

Question:- When you promised Mrs Casey on the telephone that you would tell your father, had you not at that stage your mind made up not to tell him?

Answer:- No. I was trying to work about it.

Question:- You wouldn't be averse [sic] in making a promise to a person even though you were not sure if you were going to fulfil that promise?

Answer:- I didn't feel it was up to Mrs. Casey to tell me what to do or who to tell about my problems.

Question:- You were not candid enough to say that to her on the telephone?

Answer:- My mind was not just made up at the time. I just didn't.

'Not candid enough.' 'You wouldn't be averse [sic] in making a promise to a person even though you were not sure if you were going to fulfil that promise?' I could feel the blood rushing to my face as I became more and more angry and humiliated. It was beyond anything I could have imagined: question after question being fired at me by these men of rank, each more invasive than the last.

Question:- Did you become pregnant deliberately?

Answer:- Why should someone want to become pregnant deliberately?

Question:- Did you want to hold on to Fintan Casey while you were in Templemore?

Answer:- Well, I liked him.

Question:- Did you have a physical relationship with him in Dublin before he joined the Guards?

Answer:- Yes.

Question:- Were contraceptives used by you in that first relationship?

Answer:- Yes.

Question:- Was there a question of contraceptives not being used in Shandon Road?

Answer:- Not that I can recall.

Question:- Did you not feel that you would become pregnant as a result of having sexual relations with Fintan?

Answer:- He used contraceptives.

Question:- How did this pregnancy occur if contraceptives were used?

Answer:- He did not use them the night I got pregnant.

Question:- Was that at your suggestion?

Answer:- No.

Question:- Did you use contraceptives in your relationship in 1980?

Answer:- No.

Question by Superintendent Boyle:-

Question:- Did you have sexual intercourse
    with any other person from the time you had
    sexual intercourse with Fintan Casey at 32,
    Shandon Road, Phibsboro?

Answer:- No.

Question by Garda Lawless:-

Question:- Were the initials of the surname and
    the initials of the Christian name of the
    person you had a relationship with in 1980
    the same?

Answer:- Yes.

Question:- Is it C.M.?

Answer:- Yes.

By the end of those questions, I was sobbing. I felt
embarrassed, ashamed and utterly alone. I wanted
the degradation to end, and so when I was asked
by Garda Lawless whether there was any pressure
applied to me to give David up for adoption I simply
said, 'There was no pressure.' I knew if I said that I
had been browbeaten into having my child adopted,
more and more questions would have come back at

me and I simply couldn't take any more. My child was gone now and there was nothing anyone in that room could have done to bring him back. It hardly seemed to matter whether I acknowledged the truth of what had happened.

Then came the final insult. As it is recorded in the transcript of the sworn inquiry, the interaction went as follows:

Question:- Did you pick the name yourself for the child?

Answer:- Yes, I did.

Question:- Why did you pick that name?

Answer:- I called it after the Star of David. I have also given a reply that 'I don't know, I don't know any David', the reason I gave that reply is because I felt that Garda Lawless was suggesting I called the child after somebody I knew.

In fact, Garda Lawless stated quite matter-of-factly that I hadn't called my son 'David' after the Star of David at all and that I had actually named him after a past lover.

They destroyed me in that room. Any remnant of dignity I had left, they took it from me. It was as though I had been tried by every single one of those men and found to be a promiscuous, lying slut. I felt like I was dirt on that chair and that I had deserved every moment of that humiliation. When they were finished, not for the first time, I just wanted to die.

I emerged like a woman in a trance. It seemed as though I had been questioned for hours, though, in reality, it could only have been about forty-five minutes. After I came out, the inspector went in. I was in no state to do anything but wait for her to finish and was grateful for the silence and solitude of the waiting room.

She had been in with them for about a quarter of an hour when my superintendent from Store Street, Tommy O'Reilly, arrived in the waiting room and sat down beside me. I collected myself sufficiently to make polite conversation but we both knew why he was there and what he would be discussing in the room across the corridor. We passed an awkward few minutes together before the inspector came out and Tommy was called in. And then it was time to go home. For the entire journey back to Dublin, I didn't speak.

I have never truly recovered from the events of that terrible day. I often wonder what those senior gardaí thought would be the outcome of something so ferocious; how they could justify putting a twenty-two-year-old woman in a room full of men to be torn apart the way I was. I have sat through cases in the High Court, I have sat through cases in the Circuit Court and I have sat through cases in the District Court and I have never heard a cross-examination like the one I heard in Letterkenny garda station.

When I received my garda file many years later, I learned that the doctor I had visited in Cavan, while staying with my sister in the early weeks of my maternity leave, had also been summoned to testify before the sworn inquiry. That doctor had issued two medical certificates to me on 16 February 1984, one to say I was pregnant with an estimated due date of 21 May 1984, the second to say I had viremia and a urinary tract infection. He was asked the following questions by Garda Lawless:

Question:- 'Viremia' [is] a virus infection?

Answer:- Yes.

Question:- 'UTI', is it related to the virus infection?

Answer:- Yes.

Question:- Is there any specific cause for 'Viremia' or the 'UTI'?

Answer:- There is no specific cause.

Question:- Would it be influenced by the lifestyle of the person?

Answer:- No.

Question:- How did you arrive at the expected delivery date?

Answer:- From information given to me by
Majella Moynihan and, as far as I can recall,
from clinical examinations, which concurred
with the information supplied. From the
information given to me and from experience
and a clinical examination I fixed the 21/5/84
as the likely date for delivery.

Question:- Would you be able to tell us the rough
date of when this child was likely conceived?

Answer:- I would say that it would be about mid
August, 1983.

Question:- You could not be more specific?

Answer:- I would say that it was the week
beginning the 14/8/83 from the dates supplied.

Garda Lawless's final summation to the sworn inquiry
was also in my file. Although much of it was redacted,
what remained made me sick to my stomach:

B/Garda M. Moynihan did not know if she was
in ▇▇▇▇▇▇ in August 1983 when the alleged
intercourse which would result in pregnancy
took place. She expressed doubts about the
dates she visited Donegal and volunteered the
information that she had sexual relations with
another person in 1980.

In general, she portrayed herself as a person who enjoyed the good life in Templemore. She remarked that 'all you can do down there is go to the pub'. She attended passing out parties in the Templemore Arms Hotel whether invited or not. When difficulties as a result of this showed, she picked Fintan Casey to carry the can because she believed he was the person most likely to fulfil her dreams of home and friendship.

She, the bangharda, could not explain why she did not become pregnant on that and other occasions when intercourse was alleged to have taken place.

Further examination revealed that the young lady in question was not adverse in making promises she did not intend to keep and that she had strong sexual desires.

B/Garda Moynihan lacked the necessary credibility and the charge could not be sustained at Law because the evidence offered in corroboration would be in total conflict with the standard of proof necessary in civil cases and particularly in the matter of the Illegitimate Children (Affiliation No. 17) Orders Act 1930.

In the end, it was decided that Fintan would receive a fine of £90. He was not dismissed from An Garda Síochána.

22

Surviving not living

The sworn inquiry had absorbed my attention entirely during the final weeks of April and so it never occurred to me that, just two days before it took place, I had become a fully fledged member of the force. On 27 April 1985, my two years' probation came to an end and I was appointed, automatically and without ceremony, to An Garda Síochána.

I later read a letter of recommendation that Inspector Bernard Haughey had written, prior to my confirmation, to Superintendent Tommy O'Reilly:

Re: Recruit Bangharda Abina M. Moynihan, 00338G, Store Street Station, D.M.A.

I have found R/Bangharda Moynihan to be

exceptionally honest, and always accepts full responsibility for her mistakes. She is most respectful to her superiors and anxious to learn and give a good work performance.

I have been impressed with her attitude to events arising from her pregnancy, in that, while she was emotionally upset at times, she was determined that this was not going to unduly affect her performing her duties.

In my view, this member's honesty, willingness and general attitude to her job, which has been consistent since her arrival in Store Street, outweighs the mistakes she has made in the past and accordingly I recommend that her appointment to the Force be confirmed.

Signed: Bernard Haughey, Inspector

I was surprised that the inspector noted that my state of mind during those months had not impacted on my work. When I think back to that time, I remember a woman whose misery must have been apparent to everyone she met. I was not living at all, only surviving. I hated myself – I thought I was an immoral and irresponsible person, who lacked the character and integrity to be a guard. I felt unworthy of my job, unworthy of respect and unworthy of love. My thoughts circled constantly around the events of the previous eighteen months – the disgrace of my pregnancy, the loss of David, the humiliation of the sworn inquiry – and I was entirely disengaged from the world around me.

I drank heavily through that period. I drank to suppress my feelings of guilt and shame; to try to block out the memories of all that had happened. When I was drunk, I cried for my child. More than once, I came home from a night out drinking and took a handful of paracetamol tablets before going to bed, hoping that I wouldn't wake up.

It was a long time before I could separate my own thoughts about myself and my abilities as a guard from the reality of how I went about my duties – and grant myself my due: that despite it all, I always did my job to the best of my ability, conducting myself with skill, integrity and empathy, respectful in all my dealings and indeed a garda who garnered a great deal of respect from the public.

Even through the bleakest of times to follow, my sense of duty prevailed, and once I put on that uniform, I was a guardian of the peace regardless of what was going on in my personal life. Although there were times on the beat when I would go down to Henry Place or Moore Lane and cry, just broken and wondering how I would get through it all. But I *was* getting through it – and in all my time, I was never reprimanded for my work.

Back then, however, I was too mired in shame to recognise that I had anything to be proud of.

In Store Street, it was business as usual. Of course, there was never any suggestion of my being promoted or advanced. I did the same work day in, day out and felt lucky to have a job at all.

There was no further discussion of my case. Or there wasn't to my face, at least, though I suspected that, wherever I went and whenever I was spoken of, I was given the epithet 'the one who caused all the trouble'. Sometimes, in the pub or on a night out, a guard who had had too much to drink would approach me and ask me if it was true that I'd had a baby but no one ever joked about it, which was something, because they joked about everything else.

Slagging and banter were ritual behaviours within the guards and a constant feature of the working day. You were 'one of the lads' if it was known that you could take a joke and it was very important to be one of the lads if you wanted to get ahead, especially as a woman. When a woman *did* get ahead, for instance, when a bangharda progressed to the rank of sergeant, the question was always asked: 'Who do you think *she* was sleeping with?' A favourite insult for a woman was that she was 'easy' and, as was the case elsewhere in society, a man with a reputation for sexual promiscuity was a 'stud' and a woman with the same reputation was a 'slut'. As the first bangharda from Store Street ever to have had a child outside marriage, whose sexual history was a matter of public record, I felt I was an object of ridicule.

It was a challenging workplace for any woman. By 1986, there were still only eleven banghardaí in Store Street, as opposed to 160 men, and only one woman of senior rank in the station. Even the title 'bangharda' set us apart. We were a small minority of a force whose attitudes and ethos were overwhelmingly male. On more than one occasion, after I took a statement from a victim of rape or incest or sexual harassment, I later discovered guards in Store Street reading through the statement and jeering at it. On another occasion, a bangharda whose baby was sick called in to her sergeant and requested a day's emergency leave. When she came in the following day, the sergeant took her aside and said, 'You bitch, don't you ever leave me in the lurch again.'

One evening, a gang of us from Store Street went over to Keating's pub for a few drinks after work. Towards closing time, an officer approached me and offered me a lift home. I didn't know him except by name but I knew that I lived en route to his home. Several other guards were giving or taking lifts and, besides, the officer was married and we were virtual strangers, so I assumed that there could be no harm in it.

He was parked in Store Street, so we walked across the road together and went into the car park. Our conversation, when we spoke at all, was unremarkable. When he pulled up around the corner from my father's house, I thanked him for the lift and opened the door to get out. 'It was lovely to chat to you,' I said.

'Lovely, was it?' he said, 'Well, what are you rushing off for, in that case?' He undid the fly of his trousers and pulled out his penis. 'Isn't that lovely, now?' he said, then he grabbed the back of my head and pushed my face down towards his crotch.

Even now, it turns my stomach to think about it: a married man, decades my senior, and stinking of cigarettes and stout, believing this was an appropriate way to behave with a young female colleague. He thought he could do what he liked with me and I knew that it was because he assumed that I was 'easy'. I pushed back against his meaty hand, pulled myself up and hit him in the face. 'You're nothing but a bastard,' I hissed at him, jumping from the car. I slammed the door and ran home.

I walked into my father's house, red-faced and flustered, with tears in my eyes, relieved to find that everyone was in bed. I cried myself to sleep that night and wondered when I would reach the limits of what the guards were willing to subject me to.

In Store Street, the following morning, as I was walking upstairs to the bangharda room, he was coming down the stairs. When he saw me, he laughed in my face. 'There she is, now!' he said, guffawing to himself and shaking his head. As though he had found me out. As though he had had a go of the loose woman in the station and discovered she wasn't all she was cracked up to be. What was the point of keeping a slut like that on the payroll if she wouldn't deign to give you head on demand?

I knew if I'd made a complaint, it would have been regarded as troublemaking. I could well imagine what would be said on the subject: 'A woman like that? You'd think she was a virgin, the fuss she was making. And he a family man. Would she not have some consideration for his wife at home? And what was she doing accepting a lift from a man anyway? With her reputation?'

A deep unease had settled on me. In becoming pregnant outside marriage, in having my baby, I had transgressed, and now, it seemed, my fate was sealed. I could be considered fair game.

23

Branded

In 1988, I left Store Street. The guards were piloting a computerised system for logging files and sharing data between police stations – a basic version of the modern PULSE system – and four officers were required to move to the Dublin divisional headquarters in Harcourt Square to get it up and running. Although I hadn't requested a transfer or applied for the job, I was told I would be filling one of the positions. I was convinced I had been chosen for relocation because the senior guards in Store Street had had enough of me. The traumas of the preceding years had taken a toll on my mental health and I bore little resemblance to the young woman who had joined the force in 1983. I was depressed and anxious and there could be no doubt that my performance on the job was suffering as a result.

I had several objections to the move: I hated the idea of working in an office – I had joined the guards to spend my days out on the streets, meeting people – and I was nervous at the thought of leaving the familiar surroundings of Store Street. But, since it seemed I didn't have a choice in the matter, I hoped that, if I had to leave my friends and my comfort zone, maybe I could leave my past behind me too.

In the spring of 1988, I started work in Harcourt Square. The four of us who had been selected to implement the pilot system – two guards and two banghardaí – shared a large office together on the second floor. Our days were spent inputting forms – declarations of theft, that kind of thing – into a computer in order to create a database.

I was surprised to discover that I enjoyed the repetitive, clerical task, which was so undemanding compared with the work of a garda on the beat. The atmosphere among the team was pleasant and collegial and, for the first time in years, I felt I was neither being observed nor talked about. The other bangharda, a woman named Karen, had come from Pearse Street garda station. She had also had a child outside of marriage but she had kept her baby, a little boy. She often mentioned her son but we never discussed how she had been treated by the force during and after her pregnancy, nor did we discuss my own experience.

I hadn't been in Harcourt Square very long when I ran into my old superintendent, Tommy O'Reilly. Since our dealings in 1984, when I had met with him to discuss my pregnancy and maternity leave, and in 1985, when he had made a statement about me to the sworn inquiry in Letterkenny, Tommy had received two significant promotions: the first to Chief Superintendent and the second to Assistant Commissioner, Dublin Metropolitan Area. As an assistant commissioner, Tommy was a member of the Senior Leadership team of An Garda Síochána and one of the most powerful members of the entire organisation. He and two other senior guards – Deputy Commissioner Patrick Mulligan and Assistant Commissioner P.J. Moran – were referred to as 'the three wise men', appointed to modernise the force after the guards were criticised for their handling of a number of high profile cases, including the notorious Kerry Babies investigation. He was now permanently based in Harcourt Square.

The assistant commissioner invited me into his office for a cup of tea. I liked Tommy and felt he had been kinder to me in 1984 than would have been strictly necessary, so I welcomed the catch-up.

'How have you been getting on?' he asked when we sat down.

'Not very well, Tommy, to be honest,' I told him. 'Do

you not like Harcourt Square?' he pressed. 'I suppose it's a change from Store Street. It's a bigger station and more anonymous here.' 'It's not the transfer,' I replied. 'I'm still not over everything that happened four years ago, how the guards treated me.' Tommy nodded and was silent. Having dared to bring up my case, I decided I would quiz him on a point that had been bothering me: 'Is my pregnancy on my personal file?' I asked. Tommy said that it was and then, to my surprise, he added, 'I'll have it removed, Majella.'

At first, I was delighted at the thought that the whole affair could be expunged forever. But it occurred to me, then, that, no matter what information was or wasn't on my file, gossip always travelled within An Garda Síochána. When a guard or bangharda was transferred to another station, the superintendent would often ring around to find out what there was to know about this interloper. By the time the newcomer actually arrived at the station, every aspect of his or her professional and personal life that was known within the organisation would have been discovered and discussed.

'Will it follow me anyway, Tommy?' I asked. He looked at me for a moment, as though ruminating on my situation and the extent to which I should be appraised of it. At last he sighed and said, 'It will always follow you, Majella, because guards talk. You will never get on in An Garda Síochána because of your history.'

His words hit me hard. Although I had suspected my career might suffer as a result of my pregnancy and all that came afterwards, it was shocking to receive absolute confirmation, from a source that could not be doubted, that my supposed transgressions would never be forgotten; that the garda authorities continued to regard me as having discredited the force; and that, so long as I remained within An Garda Síochána, my reputation would always go before me and would never be restored. In saying as much, Tommy wasn't being nasty, he was being realistic. He knew the organisation because he had come up through the ranks and he was telling me, frankly and honestly, where I stood.

I don't know what I said in response or how I managed to continue my side of the conversation, but when it was over I walked out of the assistant commissioner's office and returned to my desk like a condemned woman.

My first instinct was to hand in my notice. The thought of showing up to work, day after day, for an organisation that had so little respect for me, seemed unbearable. And yet, whenever I seriously contemplated resigning my position, the same questions arose time and again in my mind: 'Where would I go, if I quit? What would I do? And what employer would hire a woman who had been charged and disciplined by An Garda Síochána? I couldn't come up with a satisfactory answer for any of them. Though staying seemed unthinkable, leaving felt impossible.

I had recently moved into a flat in Rathgar and, when I finished work that evening, I went home and locked the door. I felt sick with shame and sadness and, with no one to talk to and nowhere to turn for support, I sought relief in the usual place: I opened a bottle of brandy and drank myself into a stupor.

My mental health deteriorated considerably after that day. I drank more, more often and alone. It was a struggle every morning to get up and go to work. I regularly called in sick and was usually absent one day every week. When I did come in, I struggled to concentrate for any length of time. I was visibly suffering and yet no one in Harcourt Square said a word about it. Had I been offered any help, I would have accepted it gratefully.

By this time, the logging process was complete, the pilot system was in operation and our four-person team had been disbanded. I was moved across the courtyard to the North Central Office, where my job was to process licences and permits. It was quickly noted that I was drinking heavily and regularly taking sick leave. 'Out last night, were we?' became the standard greeting every morning, frequently followed by 'Glad to see you made it in today, Majella.'

In August 1989, after another night on the town, I fell on my way out of the Harcourt Hotel and broke my wrist. Soon afterwards, my sergeant sat me down and said, 'The chief thinks your drinking has become a problem, Majella, and we're going to have to ask you to move on.' He asked whether I would consider transferring to the Bridewell Garda Station in Smithfield. I knew most of the guards in the Bridewell and I couldn't bear the thought of them all gossiping about me and my past and the transfer. I wanted to go to a place where I knew nobody and nobody knew me. 'I won't go to the Bridewell,' I told the sergeant. 'I'll go to Wexford.'

And that was how I ended up in Gorey.

24

Breakdown

The garda station in Gorey was built in 1932, on the site of an RIC barracks, which had been burned down by anti-treaty forces during the Civil War. By the time I moved to the town, in the autumn of 1989, the building was in need of modernisation but it was very well-staffed. Notably so, considering it served a population of little more than 3,000 people. There were four units, with four guards in each unit, as well as traffic corps, detectives and clerical staff, overseen by two sergeants, an inspector and a superintendent. Of the forty or so members in the station, there was only one bangharda – I was the second – so my arrival didn't go unnoticed. A photographer from the *Gorey Echo* was dispatched to the station to take my picture for the paper. In the photograph, I'm posing with a telephone receiver, wearing my peaked blue hat, the epitome of youth and happiness, but inside I was full of anxiety. I had moved to Wexford in order to be anonymous – the very last thing I wanted was to appear in the local newspaper.

Prior to my sudden transfer, I had contacted the guards in Gorey to see if anyone could help me find accommodation. It was arranged that I would take a room in the home of Aonghus and Sheila Lafferty, a couple in their thirties, who had two young daughters and lived in a three-bedroom house near the station. They were a lovely family and their home was beautifully kept but I was in no state to benefit from their kindness. I was in a very bad way.

It was now six years since I had discovered I was pregnant with David, five years since I had given him up for adoption and four years since the sworn inquiry in Letterkenny. I had tried to put the trauma of those events behind me, but if I thought the move away from Dublin would bring me any peace, I was soon disabused of the idea. In the absence of my friends and family, I was free to be as self-destructive as I chose. I was skinny – less than eight stone – because I wasn't eating properly and all I did in my spare time was drink – in the pub, with the guards from the station; or alone in my bedroom of the digs.

I did the minimum that was required of me on the job. I put on my uniform and walked the beat or I sat in the passenger seat of the patrol car and that was it. I made no arrests the whole time I was in Wexford. I was paranoid in the station and self-conscious walking down the town. I was convinced everybody was talking about me.

One evening, after I had been in Gorey for about three months, I went for a drink after work with some of the lads from my unit. We went to Brennan's, a pub on the Main Street that was famous for its three bars and where you could usually find at least one table entirely occupied by guards. We were later joined by one of the sergeants, who had been sitting in the lounge. I didn't know him very well but I knew his wife had died some years earlier, so I felt sorry for him and made an effort to include him in our conversation. When the pub closed at midnight, he invited us all back to his house in a nearby town. Several of the others cried off and went home but I went with the few that followed the sergeant. I was happy to avoid the solitude of my room for a little while longer and always willing to have another drink.

Back at the house, the sergeant brought out a bottle of vodka and began serving double and triple measures with 7-Up. After two drinks, my head was spinning. The sergeant saw I was drunk and getting drowsy and said he had a spare room and I was welcome to stay. I went in and lay down on the bed. When I woke, an hour later, the house was dark and silent and the sergeant was in my room, lying on top of me. His breath was warm and rancid on my face and I thought I was going to be sick. When I pushed him away, he laughed and lay back down on me but when I shoved him away a second time, he looked nettled. He said everyone knew I was gagging for it and that I was just 'a fucking tease'.

I lurched past him out of the room and out of the house and walked the six kilometres back to Gorey. I was crying and still groggy from the night before, as I stumbled along the verge. I dreaded the thought of anyone I knew seeing me on the road. I felt that they would realise at once what had happened.

Although I was angry with the sergeant, I was furious with myself. Maybe he was right and I had led him on and behaved like a tease. After all, what respectable woman would get drunk in a stranger's house? Here you are again, Majella, I thought to myself, living up to your reputation. You're nothing but a slapper.

Shortly after that awful night, I left my digs with the Laffertys. We had a wonderful relationship right to the end but I felt that a woman like me should not be around young children. I moved into a house in Clonattin with two girls my own age. For weeks, I just sat in my room and drank and cried. Eventually, on Valentine's Day 1990, one of the girls, Gillian, arrived home to find me drunk and screaming in the bathroom, with a razor blade in my hand. She called the garda station in Gorey and the guards called a GP. Gillian brought me to his surgery that night and, after speaking to me for fifteen minutes or so, the doctor told her to drive me straight to St. John of God psychiatric hospital in Dublin.

25

St. John of God's

Although I cried all the way to St. John of God's, I think I realised, even then, that I was going to the right place. It was a relief to admit that I couldn't cope anymore; that I couldn't carry on in the state of mind I was in. It was a relief, too, to be getting away from the guards.

We arrived at the hospital at two o'clock in the morning. I was still a little drunk and hardly knew what was happening to me. I was seen immediately by a nurse and then admitted. My bag and belongings were searched and anything potentially harmful was removed, then I was shown to a bedroom in St. Paul's, an admission ward for male and female patients. I lay in bed but couldn't sleep because my head was pounding. Every so often, another patient on the ward would shout or scream, which frightened me.

The following morning, I was brought to see a consultant psychiatrist for an initial assessment and evaluation. He introduced himself as Dr. Shelley and asked me to give a brief synopsis of my life. When I finished, he told me I was an emotional wreck and that I would have a lot of talking to do in the coming months. He arranged that, as part of my care plan, I would attend counselling and psychotherapy twice a week.

He also wanted to prescribe pills but I refused to take anything except multivitamin tablets. It's a little embarrassing to admit it now, at a time when anti-depressants are such a commonly used and vital treatment for a range of mental health conditions, but I was afraid to take them. I believed that, if I allowed myself to be medicated at all, I would be medicated forever. I had spent years using alcohol to try to block out emotions and memories and, for once in my life, I wanted to feel and remember everything. I was also fearful of the stigma around anti-depressants, which was still prevalent back then. As far as I was aware, I had never known anyone who had had to take tablets for a mood disorder and it felt too much like admitting I was broken, just as I was beginning to feel that I might one day be 'fixed'.

For the first few weeks, I stayed in a single room

in St. Paul's. I was regarded as a suicide risk, so I was kept under Level 2 observation, which meant checks every thirty minutes throughout the day and night and I was not permitted to leave the ward. There was a nurses' station at the end of the corridor, with as many as five nurses on duty during the day, so there was always someone available if you wanted to talk. Meals were served in a dining room on the ward. I was told that, if I went along with my programme and behaved well, I would be moved to another ward, St. Bridget's, where I would have more freedom of movement and could go to the coffee shop. I hated the fact that my comings and goings were being curtailed, so I decided I would follow every instruction to the letter, in the hope of securing more privileges.

In my sessions with Dr. Shelley, I talked about my childhood and the loss of my mother; about my father's abandonment of me and my sisters; and about the experience of growing up in the industrial school. I spoke about Sr. Agnes and how she had bullied me when I was a teenager. I discussed An Garda Síochána and their treatment of me, as an organisation, as well as the behaviour of individual guards. I said things to Dr. Shelley that I had never said to another human being and it was such a release to get it all out there and describe what I had been through. I was struck by how much I had suffered and all that I had survived. Having avoided doing so for years, I now confronted the events of my life and how so many of them had warped my self-image and damaged my self-esteem. Dr. Shelley listened to me without judgement and, gradually, I built up my confidence.

The whole day ran to a schedule. As well as counselling and psychotherapy, I also attended art therapy and occupational therapy and went for walks in the grounds. The staff were very gentle on me, though, and if I didn't feel like going to a session, I was never forced to go. We were encouraged to write and keep a journal, which I did and I found the practice very helpful.

After a fortnight, I was allowed to move to St. Bridget's. I was placed in a room with another young woman from Cork and, from the very start, we hit it off. She was six or seven years older than me, and, although the details of our lives were different, I felt we had so much in common. She was a wages clerk for a big company in Dublin and she was being bullied very badly at work. As a result, she was plagued by the same insecurities that I had and she had been hospitalised with depression. Some evenings, the two of us would lie on our beds and talk about the things that had been done to us and just cry and cry. When we were finished, we'd hug and laugh and one of us would say, 'They're all just a shower of bastards.' 'Bastards, the lot of them,' the other would respond.

She accepted me for who I was and I accepted her

for who she was; she helped my recovery and I helped hers.

The hours I spent in the company of other patients were some of my happiest times in St. John of God's. I had two or three group therapy sessions every week but, outside of those, we also sat in the coffee shop and shared our life stories with each other. I still remember a beautiful young man, just a few years younger than myself, who was struggling with addiction. He was a talented photographer who had studied at the Massachusetts College of Art and Design and he was the most wonderful, kind soul. I'd chat to him every afternoon over coffee and it always made my day.

There was another patient, a young woman who was suffering from post-natal depression and receiving electroconvulsive therapy. I never saw anyone benefit so much from this controversial therapy as she did. The transformation was extraordinary – it was like watching a flower bloom. I have often found that people speak about psychiatric patients with fear and revulsion and, yet, I was repeatedly struck by the gentleness of the people I met while I was in St. John of God's. I felt privileged to call them friends and it raised my spirits to see so many of them returning to themselves during the time I spent there.

After the move to St. Bridget's, I felt more like myself and capable of seeing visitors. My first visit was from Terry Hennigan, a garda welfare officer. Terry and I had worked together in Store Street and he seemed genuinely concerned for my wellbeing and interested to know whether there was anything that could be done to make things easier for me at work. I told him I was very unhappy in Wexford and Terry promised to try to arrange a new placement for me.

Kitty and her sisters came to visit every week. On one occasion, my father arrived by himself. He brought homemade scones for me and asked how I was doing. He still knew nothing about David or the actions of An Garda Síochána and assumed that my breakdown had been caused by the death of my mother and my childhood experiences in St. Joseph's. I wanted to tell him some part of what had happened to me but I didn't know where to start, so I simply said: 'Dad, I don't want to live anymore.'

I started to cry and all I wanted was for him to put his arms around me but he just couldn't do it. He sat beside me while I sobbed, until the nurses, believing he had upset me in some way, came in and asked him to leave. Kitty told me later that when my father arrived home, he said ,'Just like Margaret' over and over again. Mammy, as I have said, had been hospitalised with post-natal depression after giving birth to me, which is what had initially led to myself and my sisters being placed in care.

I stayed in the psychiatric hospital for three months. They discharged me at the end of May and I went back to Wexford but, six weeks later, I attempted suicide, this time more seriously. I was brought to Beaumont Hospital and, from there, I was sent back to St. John of God's for another two nights. I decided then, that, if I was going to get well – and I was determined that I was – I would have to stop drinking.

After my second hospitalisation in St. John of God's, I got a call from Terry Hennigan to tell me I was being transferred to Dun Laoghaire garda station, in south Dublin. 'Why Dun Laoghaire, Terry?' I asked him. 'Honestly, Majella,' he replied, 'it was the only station that would take you.'

26

A model bangharda

The station in Dun Laoghaire, which in 1990 was in Upper George's Street, was the divisional headquarters of the Dublin Metropolitan Region East. It was a huge, busy station with a staff of over one hundred guards and civil servants. Dun Laoghaire, at the time, was undergoing a period of revival. The handsome, Venetian-style Town Hall had just been re-opened, following extensive restoration and refurbishment, and there were plans in place for a new police station and courthouse to replace the existing facilities, which were shabby and outdated.

Unusually, for the time, there was a large and tight-knit group of banghardaí in the station. I found them deeply intimidating. To me, they each represented the perfect embodiment of what I could never hope to be: a model bangharda, living a model life. Whatever their flaws and tribulations may have been, I couldn't see them. My own shortcomings, I felt sure, were known to them all.

I had only been in Dun Laoghaire a matter of days when I overheard a garda in the main office refer to me as 'the slut from Store Street. The one who had the child'. I quickly gave up then on the idea of integrating into my new workplace and decided to focus on getting through each working day as best I could. I avoided conversation, where possible, and often ate lunch alone at my desk. I rarely if ever socialised or met up with anyone outside work.

For all that, the job itself required a high level of skill, and I was good at it, and recognised as such – even if I was often dragging myself into work.

One positive aspect of the transfer was the fact that it made my therapy more accessible. I was already receiving out-patient care in St. John of God Hospital, in the form of monthly counselling sessions with my psychiatrist. I also began to see a psychotherapist, Patricia Brennan in Monkstown, for 'rebirthing', an alternative therapy in which breathing techniques are used as a means of accessing repressed memories. In these sessions, which sometimes lasted two hours, the psychotherapist would instruct me in a form of shallow breathing that, if repeated quickly and consistently, would bring about an altered state of consciousness. Though the process was painful – sometimes quite literally so – I found it cathartic. Again and again, I found myself returning to my childhood feelings of abandonment and the guilt and shame I experienced as a result of my own subsequent abandonment of David. Having identified these emotions in rebirthing sessions, I would then explore them with my psychiatrist in counselling. It was a process that I found very helpful.

In 1991, I spent a week on a course with Fr. Pat Murray, a Pallottine father who had founded a therapeutic community in Athy, in a house called Galilee. There he worked alongside Sr. Miriam to help people through a combination of group therapy and Christian meditation. The course was called 'Who am I?' and I truly believe I released some of the pain of my past that week.

In the station, things were more prosaic. The computer system I had helped to pilot in Harcourt Square was now operational across An Garda Síochána and, in Dun Laoghaire, my job was, once again, to input forms and details of crimes into the database. I shared an office with a quiet, young civil servant from the Department of Justice who was engaged in the same work.

In 1992, the guards in Dun Laoghaire vacated the station in Upper George's Street and moved to a modern, purpose-built building in Corrig Avenue.

A few days before the new premises were officially unveiled, I was approached by a sergeant, who told me that the garda commissioner, Patrick Culligan, and David Andrews, a TD for Dun Laoghaire and then minister for foreign affairs, would be coming to the opening. It was planned that both men would come and inspect my office, so that I could show them the computerised database and explain to them what it did and how it worked.

I felt sick at the idea. Although Patrick Culligan was a very different man to Larry Wren, the commissioner who had sought to dismiss me in 1984, he still represented the leadership of An Garda Síochána, at whose hands I had suffered such injustice. The thought of sharing a room with him filled me with anxiety and the prospect of being inspected by him was terrifying. I felt certain that, once again, I would be weighed and found wanting.

I tried, at once, to resist the proposal and, when the chief superintendent insisted, I pleaded to be excused, saying I had no desire to be in the limelight and that anyone at all could operate the computer, if they were given some time to prepare. But the plan was settled and no volunteers came forward to take my place.

On the morning of the opening, the minister and the commissioner arrived promptly at eleven o'clock. Having walked the perimeter of the new building and admired the facade, they began their tour of the offices. When they arrived in my room, accompanied by the chief superintendent of Dun Laoghaire garda station, Des Malone, I shrank from any introduction, imagining that as soon as my name was mentioned the commissioner would realise who I was and what I had done.

A photographer came in to capture the moment when I sat down at my computer to give the assembled dignitaries a demonstration of the new system. When I saw the photograph, many years later, I was shocked by the image it presented. I saw three powerful men looming over the chair of a woman who appears thin and gaunt. There is no trace of happiness in the woman's face and no sense that she takes any pride whatsoever in her abilities or in her work. She looks like a hunted animal.

I have no idea how I managed to conduct that presentation or participate in the question-and-answer session that followed it. I can only attribute it to sheer muscle memory, force of habit and adrenaline. I wanted those men out of my office as soon as humanly possible and the fact that I managed to speak intelligibly and perform satisfactorily while they were in it is a miracle, as far as I am concerned.

The visit ended with speeches and sandwiches in the conference room, which I did not attend.

*

While I was working in Dun Laoghaire, I also sustained a serious facial injury, though not in the line of duty. I was bitten by a black Labrador that came with a visitor to the house where I had digs in Killiney. I was left with considerable scarring across the right side of my face, all the way to the eyelid, and for several months afterwards I had a twitch, which caused the eye to flick upwards. I wasn't really aware of it myself but I could see that people found it unnerving. I was out on leave, on and off, for weeks at a time.

In the months following the dog bite, I suffered from nightmares, flashbacks, panic attacks and mood swings. When the dog had lunged at me, I'd fallen back against a radiator and hit my head, and I don't know whether it was as simple as a correlation between two blows to the head against two different radiators, seventeen years apart – but I found that the incident had triggered memories of Sr. Agnes and the physical abuse she had inflicted on me in St. Joseph's.

Eventually, I sought help and came under the care of Dr. Denis Murphy, a consultant psychiatrist in Tallaght Hospital, and, later, Dr. Michael Corry, a consultant psychiatrist in the Institute of Psychosocial Medicine in Dun Laoghaire. In his notes, Michael Corry described me as:

...a sad looking withdrawn individual with sallow complexion and of average build...She complained of extreme self consciousness with respect to her facial disfigurement. In addition she complained of loss of interest in herself, feelings of anger, feelings of mistrust, a phobic avoidance of dogs, feelings of aloneness, guilt feelings, poor self esteem, loss of confidence, self blame, mood swings, weight gain, feelings of unattractiveness, feelings of unworthiness and profound feelings of alienation from those around her, in particular, her colleagues at work. With respect to the latter, she had paranoid thoughts in addition to feelings of persecution.

She complained of poor concentration, difficulty socialising, loss of her sense of humour, loss of spontaneity, difficulty dealing with responsibilities and an inability to finish what she starts.

His report makes for miserable reading and shows how much I had changed from the bright and bubbly young woman I had once been. On Dr. Corry's recommendation, having avoided and feared anti-depressants for years, I finally agreed to try Prozac, and I did find it helpful.

To improve the appearance of my face I was referred to a consultant plastic surgeon, Mr. Gerard Edwards, who opened up the wound, cleaned it and sewed it back together. He recommended that I have six sessions of laser treatment on the new scar and, by the end of those, I was greatly relieved that my scarring had been much reduced.

*

The remainder of my career as a bangharda was spent in Dun Laoghaire. For the most part, my time in that station was spent unhappily, but unremarkably. There is only one other incident that looms large in my memory, a few years into my time there. I was walking down to the public office to collect a fresh batch of forms to input into the computer system when I met another guard on the stairs. He was known to myself and my colleague for coming into the room where we worked from time to time, making lewd comments and gestures. This time, however, he went much further. As he passed me on the stairs, he put his hand out and grabbed me hard between my legs. I was shocked and upset but I just kept on walking as though nothing had happened.

I had long ago internalised that most toxic of states for a woman who has been subjected to harassment or abuse: that the shame is on you; that somehow, you were asking for it. I am glad that, with the benefit of therapy and the wisdom of years, I now see it for what it was: a deep-running misogyny that permeated the force – even if its ugliest manifestations did not extend to most working within it – where boys were allowed to be bad, and girls who were deemed not to be good were walking targets.

27

Love matters

In 1994, I met the man who would become my husband.

It was a Friday in April and I was spending the weekend at a retreat in St. Mary's Priory in Tallaght. Since my stay in St. John of God's, I had been on several retreats and I found them peaceful and restorative. They were also useful as a way to pass the time at weekends, now that I wasn't drinking anymore.

I arrived late for registration and as I hurried to give my name at the desk, a man approached me and offered to help with my bags. I was flustered and disorganised and in no mood for gallantry, so I told him, 'Thank you, no, I'm fine.' As he turned away, I noticed he had beautiful dark eyes and I felt a twinge of regret for rebuffing his kindness. I made an effort to speak to him again later in the evening and he told me his name was Martin Peelo and he was from Crumlin. When he added that he was a garda sergeant, stationed in Kevin Street, I couldn't believe it. Was I never to be free from the surveillance of An Garda Síochána? The old paranoia returned and I imagined that, if I introduced myself as a guard, the attractive stranger would identify me at once. I told him my name was Majella and I was a nurse and then I moved on to speak to some of the others in the group.

The following morning, Martin sought me out and, with a roguish look, said, 'You're not a nurse. You're a guard.' 'How do you know?' I retorted defensively. 'I asked around and some of the others know you and what you do for a living,' he told me. I felt, then, that I had been too reserved and that Martin was hurt by my deception, so I reassured him by saying that I didn't always like to tell people I was a member of the force before I had got to know them properly.

We spent a lot of time together over the weekend. Martin told me he had two young daughters and that he had been married but that he and his wife had separated that February. I felt reluctant to get involved with someone whose marriage had ended so recently, but, when he asked me to meet him for a walk the following week, I agreed. There was something very kind and paternal about him, which may have been partly explained by the fact that he was twelve years older than me, but also because I felt I could be vulnerable around him.

Martin, I discovered on our walk, was the eldest of eight and he came from a family of servicemen. His father had been a company sergeant in the Irish Army and a brother had been in the Royal Navy and, later, became a sergeant in the Hampshire Constabulary. Martin had joined the RAF when he was eighteen but left because he was homesick for his beloved Dublin. He showed me a photograph of himself and his father and brother, taken in the back garden of the family home in Crumlin, with Martin in his RAF uniform, Tony in his Royal Navy uniform and their father in his army uniform.

It was clear that Martin loved being a guard. He said, of his early days in Kevin Street station, that he would have gone into work for no money at all. He loved the camaraderie among the officers and told me he felt honoured to be policing Dublin and keeping its people safe. Martin's father had always emphasised to him the importance of taking care of the vulnerable.

I said very little about myself on that first walk. I told Martin about my childhood in Mallow and the death of my mother and talked a bit about the various stations where I had served but, beyond that, I hardly knew where to start. The story of my life didn't make for easy listening and I felt certain events might well scare off a potential partner. Martin and I had been seeing each other for about a month before I ventured to discuss my first pregnancy and all that had followed. He was shocked. He said he had read about the story in the papers and that it had been talked about a little in Kevin Street but that he hadn't realised I was the bangharda in question. My description of the sworn inquiry roused his protective instincts but when I went as far as to say 'I really hate the guards for what they have done to me,' Martin stiffened and became uncomfortable. Disloyalty of any kind was anathema to him, particularly where it related to An Garda Síochána.

It was crazy, really, for me to go out with a guard, particularly one whose allegiance to the organisation was ardent and unquestioning. From the very beginning, our opposing views on the guards were a source of strain. Had I been with anyone else, I could have ranted about the guards as much as I liked and, had Martin been with anyone else, he could have adored his job in peace. But we fell in love, and as is the way of these things, we tried our best to resolve our differences – for a time at least.

28

Death of a quiet man

In February 1996, my father died unexpectedly.

Towards the end of his life, he and I often went without seeing each other for months at a time. By this time, I was living with Martin in his flat in Walkinstown. I spoke to Kitty on the phone but I rarely visited the house in Phibsborough. It was just too hard. It wasn't that things were acrimonious between us, it was just that we had no relationship and nothing at all to say to each other and that was bad enough.

The last time I saw him was when I called over to Shandon Road, shortly before Christmas, to drop in boxes of sweets and biscuits and a bottle of whiskey for him. My father had had his lung removed in 1993 and I knew his health had been bad on and off afterwards but I was shocked when I saw how thin and frail he had become. Still, I didn't think anything was going to happen. Not so suddenly and not so soon.

On the day he died, I got a telephone call at Martin's flat from the station in Dun Laoghaire. A neighbour had left a message with the guards in the public office, asking me to go to the family home at once. 'They said it's something around your father' was all the officer would say, when I pressed him for information.

Martin drove me across the city. In the two years that we had been together, he had never met Kitty or my father. When we got to the house, Kitty answered the door. She was distraught and told me my father was already dead. He had been out walking their dog Toby and when he got back to the house he came in the side door and fell straight to the ground. Kitty called an ambulance, but when it arrived he was unresponsive. 'A massive heart attack,' the paramedic said. The Moynihans had always had heart problems. 'He would have died instantly.'

Kitty asked if I would go and identify the body – she said she couldn't bear to do it herself – so Martin and I got back into the car and drove to the Mater Hospital. I was brought down to where my father was, in the mortuary. There was a young guard in there and she showed me the body. It was awful to see him like that, lying out on a slab. He was still a fine big man but his face and body were purple. 'That's Hugh Moynihan,' I said to the guard.

A nurse took me aside and gave me his belongings – some notes and coins and a watch – and I put them in my bag to give to Kitty. Then I held his hand and said goodbye. He was seventy-one years old, and right to the end he was a stranger to me. There was so much of my life he knew nothing about and so much of his life I knew nothing about. He had five lovely daughters and he was never really a father to any of us.

Hugh Moynihan got a terrible shock when his wife Margaret died and he just ran, never to return. I don't think he gave much thought to the consequences. Industrial schools like St. Joseph's had been set up to provide for the needs of children, like his daughters, who had lost one or both parents – the option was there for him, so he took it. I imagine it was suggested to him that a man on his own couldn't cope with a house full of girls.

I used to say, 'If only he had been stronger, we would have had a home life.' But despite the consequences of this abandonment in my early life, I accept now that Dad did what he thought was best, under the circumstances.

*

Six years before he died, my father and I drove to Wexford together. I had just been released from St. John of God's, for the second time, and we were going to the house in Clonattin to collect my belongings.

Kitty had suggested I come and stay in Shandon Road for a while, until I was feeling a bit stronger.

My father and I had never been alone together, at such close quarters, for so long and the fact that I had been hospitalised twice in recent months seemed to provide a reasonable pretext for a meaningful conversation. I decided to ask him why he had put us into an orphanage.

He was thoughtful for a while, and eventually said, 'You'll never know what it's like to lose your wife and five children.'

'But you didn't lose them,' I said, 'you gave them up.'

My father didn't cry but he went very quiet. I knew not to push it any more, and our conversation ended there, never to be revisited.

29

Becoming a mother again

Once our relationship was securely established, Martin introduced me to his daughters, who were twelve and fourteen at the time. I felt so much affection for the two of them from the very beginning and I could see that this was a comfort to Martin. I remember one cold February evening, when all four of us were in the flat in Walkinstown. The girls were having baths, so I warmed their towels by the fire. It was such a small gesture but, in bed that night, Martin told me it had meant a lot to him.

We talked about having a baby. I knew I wanted one but Martin wasn't sure. He was forty-four when we met and felt he was too old to start into the child-rearing routine again. He was worried, too, about how his daughters might feel about a new addition. Discussions were ongoing for some time but the issue was resolved after two years, when I was informed by my GP that I was five weeks pregnant. Afterwards, I stood outside the surgery, hugging my belly and thinking, I'm going to mind you forever. I remembered the acerbic little line that had been delivered to me by Chief Superintendent Jim Sullivan in Harcourt Square: 'If it happens you again, Bangharda Moynihan, you're sacked.' This time, though, I had a supportive partner and was strong enough in myself to think, I will not be sacked because of this child. By God, you will not do anything to me.

Martin told his daughters early on about the baby. To his great relief, they were both very pleased to hear the news. He told me with a chuckle that, when he referred to the child as their 'half-brother or half-sister', the girls had said, 'Why the half, Da? Will it be half a baby?' Once they knew about the situation and were happy about it, Martin felt that he, too, could relax and enjoy the pregnancy.

We spared no expense when it came to my antenatal care. We had a private consultant in the Coombe Hospital and he couldn't have been more attentive. Ireland in 1997 was a very different place for unmarried mothers from what it had been in 1984, and I'm sure it helped, too, that Martin was beside me, holding my hand, the whole way through. It made me sad to compare all that comfort and tranquillity with the misery and trauma of my earlier pregnancy. Then, I'd had to hide the fact that I was expecting a baby, whereas this time I flaunted it, wearing beautiful maternity clothes and merrily putting on weight. My excitement made me feel guilty, at times, and I had to tell myself that I was a completely different person in completely different circumstances.

Stephen was born on 22 May 1997. I had gone into the Coombe the previous night with contractions and at eleven the next morning my waters were forcibly broken to induce labour. The contrast with David's birth in 1984 could not have been more marked. My obstetrician was present throughout the delivery and he made sure I was given an epidural. When my son arrived at last, at 3.15 p.m., he was placed on my chest and my heart danced. It was discovered that Stephen had a bronchial infection so he was taken away to an incubator, but I had unfettered access to him while he was receiving treatment. As long as I was awake, I was by his side – I was determined that no one would take that child anywhere without my knowledge and consent.

Stephen was baptised on 9 July in Walkinstown church. We walked to the ceremony from our new family home across the green. I held on tight to my baby in his beautiful christening gown and smiled at everyone we met on the way. When Fr. Tom welcomed my son into the family of God, I cried with joy and happiness.

Martin and I were married twice. The first time, on 14 June 2001, was in the Dublin registry office, after Martin's divorce came through. We had a reception in the Red Cow Inn and went on honeymoon to Menorca with Stephen. The second time, on 14 June 2014, we were married in the church in Walkinstown, after Martin's first marriage was annulled. My faith, at times, was the one thing that had kept me going, so it meant a lot to me to have a real church wedding. For the first time in a long time, I felt hopeful for the future.

30

The great escape

I had had a blissful year of maternity leave after Stephen was born. I disappeared entirely into family life – cooking and baking for Martin and the baby and decorating our new home. I revelled in every aspect of motherhood, relishing each tiny experience that had previously been denied to me. At last I felt loved. At last I felt worthy. At last I had a purpose.

I dreaded any interruption of this domestic bliss but there was the mortgage to consider and improvements still to be made to the house, so after Stephen's first birthday I enrolled him in a crèche in Walkinstown and returned to Dun Laoghaire, where I was to be deployed as a community guard. Community policing back then involved maintaining a visible presence in the area, working with organisations like Neighbourhood Watch to keep Dun Laoghaire safe, and establishing positive relationships with local residents. A lot of my time was spent visiting the elderly in the old folks' home in Monkstown and bringing children from the nearby Cottage Home residential care facility out on trips. It was exactly the sort of work I had joined the guards to do and I should have felt fulfilled, but instead I just felt numb.

Returning to work had meant a return to the same oppressive working environment. I felt as alienated as ever from my colleagues and just as resentful of the institution. That year, I was back in counselling and the focus, in those sessions, was very much on the events of 1983–5. I was reliving the degradation that had been meted out to me during those years, only to get up the following morning and go into work for the organisation that had treated me so shamefully. My mental health began to deteriorate and I found myself slipping back into my old ways of thinking. One night as I lay awake in bed I started to contemplate suicide and that was when I decided enough was enough: I was getting out.

I knew that quitting the guards would have consequences. For one thing, I was bound to suffer a substantial loss of earnings. But I had a family now and could no longer pretend that each day I spent in uniform wasn't damaging me and blighting our chances of happiness. If I had stayed, I would have died, and I was determined to live for Martin and Stephen.

I spoke to a bangharda in the welfare section and told her that I was stressed and miserable and wanted to leave. She arranged with garda headquarters to have my resignation papers sent to the station. The guards in Dun Laoghaire were shocked when they heard what I was doing. I remember one sergeant shaking his head in astonishment: 'You're leaving behind a good, pensionable job,' he said. I just shrugged. As far as I was concerned, all I was leaving behind was bad memories.

I was sent to the garda surgeon for a final medical examination and, after that, I was ready to go.

On 4 September I was called into the office of the chief superintendent and told that the forms had arrived from garda headquarters for me to sign. Inside was a half sheet, stating that I was being discharged on medical grounds. The letter didn't elaborate on the nature of the condition from which I had been deemed to be suffering; it merely informed me that, as a result, I would be receiving only half of my pension and half of my gratuity – a once-off payment received by gardaí departing the force, which typically amounted to one-and-a-half times their salary. I was stunned, but, at that point, there was no turning back. I quickly calculated that the income would just about cover my mortgage, then comforted myself with the thought that half a pension was better than no pension at all.

When I walked out of the station I felt weightless. At last I had regained my identity and my liberty. I was saddened by the thought that I hadn't lived out my childhood dream but that was nothing compared with the satisfaction derived from turning my back on an organisation that had turned its back on me.

It was the best decision I ever made.

*

As the months went by, I became more and more curious about the medical reasons for my discharge and reduced pension. I hired a solicitor, James Flynn, who contacted An Garda Síochána and the Department of Justice, Equality and Law Reform on my behalf, requesting confirmation of the exact condition from which I was deemed to be suffering.

He received the following reply:

Department of Justice, Equality and Law Reform
51 St. Stephen's Green,
Dublin 2,

Dear Sir,
I am to advise that the Garda Surgeon has certified that your client is so incapacitated by infirmity of mind that she is unable to perform the duties as a member of the Garda Síochána and that incapacity is likely to be permanent

*and on that basis she was discharged from the
force in accordance with the Garda Síochána
(Retirement) Regulations 1934 with effect from
the 4th September 1998.*

'Incapacitated by infirmity of mind.' From the
moment I read those words I knew that no matter
what happened in the future, I would never be able
to ask for a reference from An Garda Síochána. Who
would ever employ a woman who had been described
in such a way, especially when the stated 'incapacity'
was believed to be permanent? The basis for that belief
was later laid out in a letter to my solicitor from the
garda surgeon.

*Garda Headquarters,
Phoenix Park, Dublin 8
Re: Ex-Garda Abina Majella Moynihan, 00338G*

*Garda Majella Moynihan was examined by me
on 21/7/98 and was diagnosed as suffering from
chronic depression and was so incapacitated by
her infirmity that I was of the opinion that she
was unable to perform her duties and that this
incapacity was likely to be permanent.*

*Please refer to her consultant psychiatrist's reports
of Doctor M. Corry et al for details in depth.*
G. McCarthy
Consultant Physician Garda Surgeon

Dr. Michael Corry was the consultant psychiatrist who had treated me after the dog bite and I can only assume that the report he wrote about me at that time formed the basis for the garda surgeon's diagnosis of chronic depression.

In 2003 and 2004, I returned to Dr. Corry for a second evaluation and, in his subsequent report, he presented the following opinion of me. I have always found it very moving.

> It is a fact that, given the uniqueness of the self, a description of what an individual such as Majella [Moynihan] experienced is not just linguistically complex but beyond the domain of language itself. How can one describe the experience of distress, and turmoil in the face of uncontrollable stress, deprivation and wilful abuse both verbal and physical. Likewise I find myself equally challenged to convey within the terminology of psychiatry sadness, misery, fear, self-loathing, unhappiness, isolation, which impacted on her from an early age. I feel the greatest damage inflicted upon her arose out of the manner in which she was perceived. It is my opinion that one of the most fundamental laws of consciousness relates to the notion that; how we are perceived by others dictates how we perceive ourselves. In other words, if a child

such as Majella is told 'Majella you're no good, Majella you're no good', the child will ultimately internalise it and relate to themselves in a manner far worse than the most ruthless enemy could be imagined to do so. As mentioned above such was her depth of self-loathing that she desired more than anything the taking of her own life.

With respect to her future wellbeing, it is my opinion that a setback, even minor by objective standards, has the possibility of activating or igniting deep-seated vulnerabilities and cause an enormous impact as her system at the psycho-neurochemical levels is already primed. Consequently my prognosis is guarded. Her trauma remains unresolved. It is best described as an unresolved post traumatic stress disorder. Ongoing careful monitoring is indicated and the availability of adequate psychological services crucial.

Michael Corry

Consultant Psychiatrist in Rehabilitation Medicine

31

Meeting my son

When a child is taken from you and sent to live elsewhere, not a day goes by in which you don't think of him. You wonder what you would be doing together if you had been able to keep him. You picture what he would be like if he had stayed with you. You imagine all the concerns that would fill your days, your weeks and your life – a grazed knee, an unrequited crush, a dreaded exam, a parent–teacher meeting. Losing a child to adoption creates a hundred little holes that can never be filled.

When Stephen was ten, I told him that he had a brother, who had been given up for adoption. 'What's adoption?' Stephen asked. I explained what it meant and told Stephen that, if he had any questions, he could come to me at any time. He had only one question: 'Am I the only child of you and Daddy?' I assured him that he was.

After David went to his new family, I stayed in touch with Sr. Mary Lillis, the social worker from Clarecare, who had overseen his adoption. I called her every few months and sent cards and letters to her to send on to my son, and she would reply from time to time.

21st May, 1993

Dear Majella,
What a surprise to hear from you. The couple who have adopted David are working in Africa for the last few years. I am writing to them at the address of the Irish Company which has employed them to make contact with me when they come home in the Summer.
I am not sure how long all this will take or if I'll be able to get a photograph but I'll see what I can do. I'll certainly be able to get up-to-date information.
Sincerely,
Mary Lillis (Sr.)
Social Worker

Date not included or visible

Dear Majella,
Thank you for your card which I received some

time ago. *I have now made contact with David's adoptive parents and visited them and met David. I will be in Dublin on Friday 13th and I was wondering if it would be possible for us to meet. I will be finishing a meeting in Marlborough Street at 2 p.m. approximately. Could we meet after that? Please ring or write and let me know. If I'm not at above number you can leave a message about time and place for a meeting. Best wishes and looking forward to hearing from you.*

  Mary Lillis (Sr.)
  Social Worker

26ᵗʰ August, 1993

Dear Majella,
Can I tell you how delighted I was to meet you the last time I was in Dublin?

  I'm sending you on information in writing on David just in case you've forgotten the details.

  He is of average height, has no extra weight.

  He has light brown hair.

  He has an outgoing personality. He is a good mixer with other children and he likes to be in charge. He also gets on well with adults.

  He is highly intelligent and is more prepared to study than he used to be.

  Regarding health, he has had his appendix removed.

He has a great appetite and loves large quantities of food without sauces.

He is interested in football and karate.

So that's all the information on David. I will be delivering the photographs of you in about 2 weeks' time, if there's anything you would like me to say to David's adoptive parents, that you forgot to say 2 weeks ago.

Best wishes,

Mary Lillis (Sr.)

Social Worker

I often requested photos of him, though there weren't many forthcoming because, in 1988, David and his family had left Ireland to go and live in Africa. I was aware that they had emigrated and, every so often, Sr. Mary Lillis would contact me and let me know how David was getting on in his new home but there were long periods of time when I heard nothing at all. In August 1993, I met with Mary Lillis and expressed to her how much I regretted ever having given David up. I told her I regarded the adoption as a forced adoption and that I blamed An Garda Síochána for the decision because of the undue pressure they had placed on me from the moment I had informed them that I was pregnant. Mary was sympathetic and told me she would take a note of my comments but it was apparent that, as far as she was concerned, David had gone to a better place.

In 2005, a younger social worker, Laura O'Callaghan, took over my case. I now received regular updates about David and his life. I told Laura I would love to meet him and she said that she would let me know if David ever expressed the same wish.

Seven years later, in 2012, Laura told me that David was interested in arranging a meeting. I was so happy. I knew that reunions between birth mothers and their children could be complicated but I couldn't help picturing the fairy tale scenario. Again and again, in the days leading up to our meeting, I imagined perfect scenes of love and reconciliation, in which I apologised to David for having abandoned him and he forgave me at once, before the two of us set about making up for the time that had been lost and became integrated into each other's lives and families.

Laura could sense that I had high expectations and didn't want me to get hurt. She arranged for David and I to meet in the Berkeley Court Hotel on Lansdowne Road in Ballsbridge, and suggested that she and I have a coffee in the lobby of the hotel beforehand, so that she could give me a sense of what might happen. 'It's not going to be an easy meeting,' she warned me, when I sat down with her that morning. 'You have to remember,' she said, 'that even though you're his birth mother and he's your son, you're strangers to each other.' It was good advice but I don't think I absorbed a single word.

When David walked into the room, I was so startled by his resemblance to me that I burst into tears. Even his eyes were the same colour as mine. When he was born, he had been the image of Fintan but now here he was, a pure Moynihan. I held him by the shoulders and looked into his face. 'I'm so sorry,' I said.

He shook his head. 'There's no need to be sorry,' he replied.

Then we hugged. In that moment, it felt as though my son had returned to me.

We sat down beside each other on the couch and ordered coffee and sandwiches. David told me he was a mature student, studying English in Trinity, and living in Dublin. He told me about where he had gone to school in Clare and the years he had spent in Africa. I just kept looking at him and crying. Laura had told me to try to be authentic but I was nervous around my lost boy and afraid to be myself. I was anxious about saying the wrong thing and causing offence, so I ran every thought through a dozen filters and hardly uttered a word. I didn't want to overwhelm him, in our first meeting, with the details of his birth and adoption, so I said very little on the subject. I had brought the album that I had kept with me through the years, with the picture of myself and David together in Galway; the photographs that Biddy, David's foster mother, had taken of him in Ennis; and the ones that Sr. Mary Lillis had passed on to me from his adoptive parents. I started to talk through the album with David but, as it went on, I realised that I had no idea who I was to this twenty-seven-year-old man sitting in front of me. I could speak to him very simply about my parents and my sisters or tell him about Martin and Stephen but I couldn't put my arm around him.

The conversation dwindled and David said he had to go. We agreed that we would arrange to meet up again through the social worker. The meeting had lasted little more than an hour. When I left the hotel, I was drained. I got into my car and cried all the way home.

Many years later, I attended a course for birth mothers in Barnardos and everyone said the same thing: the hardest thing you'll ever have to do is meet your child. It's supposed to be a happy day, but in reality an event you hope will be filled with love is filled with guilt for you and pain for them. I was upset that my boy was now a man and that he had grown up without me. I wanted that baby back in my arms. I wanted the two of us to start afresh. If I could live my life all over again and change only one thing, I know that I would keep my son.

32

An unguarded life

On Saturday, 15 June 2019, I sat down in my kitchen in Walkinstown with a group of friends and family and heard my life story go out on the national airwaves in a powerful documentary on RTÉ Radio 1. After thirty-four years, it was an extraordinary, cleansing experience to tell the country what I had been subjected to as a vulnerable young woman in An Garda Síochána. Every one of us in that room was in tears from the moment the voiceover began:

On the 6th February 1985, a story made the lead in both the *Irish Times* and the *Irish Independent*. An unnamed garda – a bangharda, as she would have been called then – was being threatened with dismissal from the force, for having had premarital sex with another probationary garda and for having given birth to a baby outside wedlock...

That broadcast was more than two years in the making.

In 2017, a friend, Susan Lohan of the Adoption Rights Alliance, had introduced me to Aoife Kelleher, a journalist and filmmaker. Aoife had previously directed a number of high-profile documentaries for RTÉ and Susan thought she might be interested in my story. That March, the three of us sat down together in the Mont Clare Hotel on Merrion Street and talked about my treatment at the hands of the garda authorities and the forced adoption of my son, David. Aoife was appalled by what I told her and astonished at my resilience. She brought the story to Liam O'Brien and Sarah Blake of RTÉ's *Documentary on One* team and together the three of them set about making the radio programme that would focus national attention on my ordeal.

The team used documents I had in my possession to piece together the events that took place during my time as a member of An Garda Síochána and establish what decisions had been made in relation to me and my case and who was involved. Over the years, I had assembled a dossier relating to my pregnancy and David's adoption; the sworn inquiry; my treatment for my subsequent depression and, eventually, my discharge from the force. I knew I had been mistreated by the guards and was determined that, as soon as the opportunity arose, I would tell my story. The dossier also including my internal garda file, which had been released to me by the force in 2009, though much of the material had been redacted.

When we began the process of making the documentary, I sought more complete access to my file, under data protection legislation, but was told by the guards that the unredacted versions could not be provided because my file had gone missing. No one from the guards has ever clarified how my file could have been lost or destroyed, nor, to my knowledge has any attempt ever been made to reconstruct the file. Nevertheless, the documents I *did* manage to assemble were an invaluable resource and, combined with archive and interviews, the programme provided a vivid account of the injustice I'd suffered.

When it ended, I felt unburdened. At last my truth was out there. At last the reckoning had come. I had kept my secrets for so many years and now they were no longer my shame; they were other people's shame.

The response to the documentary, when it went out, was instantaneous and overwhelming. Within hours, the garda commissioner, Drew Harris, had apologised to me in an official statement: 'On behalf of An Garda Síochána,' he said, 'I fully apologise to former garda Majella Moynihan for the manner in which she was treated and the subsequent lifelong impact this had on her.'

I felt vindicated by the apology when it came, even if it did come thirty-four years too late and from a commissioner who had had nothing to do with my case. I wondered, though, why Drew Harris had communicated his apology in a public statement, instead of requesting to convey it in person. I felt I needed to meet the commissioner face-to-face and tell him all that I had been through and how the abuse that had been inflicted on me by the organisation, of which he was the chief representative, had changed the entire course of my life.

The morning after the broadcast, then Minister for Justice and Equality Charlie Flanagan echoed the garda commissioner's statement with his own official apology, stating: 'I sincerely regret the appalling ordeal that Ms Moynihan faced as a young garda member. The treatment she has described was simply wrong on every level. In fact, it is shocking.'

I cried when I heard Charlie Flanagan's words. To hear a sitting minister for justice say that what the guards had done to me was wrong was forceful and restorative. For more than three decades I'd had a voice in my head telling me I was dirty and disgusting and had brought discredit on the force. Now at last that voice was silent.

That Sunday evening, I was the lead story on the RTÉ

news. A reporter, Laura Hogan, came out to my house with a cameraman and filmed an interview with me in my dining room. The headline was: 'Former garda Majella Moynihan is seeking a face-to-face meeting with garda commissioner following his apology'.

On the morning of Monday, 17 June, I was interviewed on the *Today With Sean O'Rourke* programme. I found it very fulfilling that I was able to go on live radio and speak my truth. Sean O'Rourke was wonderful. I was nervous but I found him so warm, so understanding and so shocked, particularly when I told him about my suicide attempts, which were something I hadn't discussed in the documentary. While I was in the RTÉ Radio studios in Donnybrook, the news broke that the garda commissioner wanted to meet me in person to apologise.

Later that day, the Garda Representative Association issued the following statement:

> The Garda Representative Association (GRA) has today expressed its highest admiration for the dignity and bravery of former Garda Majella Moynihan who this weekend revealed details of her mistreatment at the hands of An Garda Síochána in the 1980s.
>
> In speaking publicly about her ordeal as a pregnant single woman, Majella laid bare a litany of shocking and disgraceful behaviours on

the part of the Garda Síochána – including some of her colleagues.

Majella's experience was a product of a time in which people in a position of power were influenced by social values which had profound disregard for women…

The GRA of today distances itself from any implication that Majella had done anything wrong and would robustly defend any attempt to victimise a woman on the grounds that led to the disciplinary hearing against her.

We also note the child's father was subject to a disciplinary hearing in which Majella was called as a witness, which is another disgraceful aspect of this shocking episode.

I can't say that the GRA's statement meant very much to me at all. I will never forget the terrible words of the general secretary of the association, Jack Marrinan, when he said he expected banghardaí to be 'moral in every way' and I am still very hurt at the lack of support I received from the GRA down the years. They could have done so much more for me than they did. When I needed them, they just weren't there.

On Tuesday, 18 June, then Taoiseach Leo Varadkar told the Dáil that the treatment I had received was 'deeply sexist' and 'wrong at every level'. He requested that the Minister for Justice and Equality meet with me as soon as possible.

The following day Minister for Children Katherine Zappone said she had heard the documentary and was deeply moved by my story, adding that the state must face up to how women such as former garda Majella Moynihan were treated, and make reparations for the 'terrible aspects of our past'.

On the Thursday I met with Garda Commissioner Drew Harris and Minister for Justice and Equality Charlie Flanagan, in the commissioner's office in the Phoenix Park. It was nerve-racking to return to garda headquarters after so many years but I walked into that room with my head held high and I didn't carry one ounce of shame. It was an emotional meeting and I really felt that both of those men understood the ordeal I had endured. I was very appreciative of the fact that they had taken the time to apologise to me in person and to listen to what I had to say. The following day, in a prepared statement, the commissioner said he was 'pleased to meet Ms Moynihan yesterday and offer her a fulsome apology in person on behalf of An Garda Síochána'. To me, he said that his door was always open.

In September 2019, I lodged initial papers in the High Court, via my solicitor Seán Costello, suing the Department of Justice and Equality, the garda commissioner and the Director of Public Prosecutions.

In the process, I began two legal actions against the state: the first, to recover the money I lost when my policing career was cut short, including loss of earnings over a fifteen to twenty-year period and the losses to my pension and gratuity payment; and the second, to seek personal injury compensation for the trauma and the harm that was done to me.

That documentary brought so many people back into my life. For months afterwards, I was contacted by old friends and schoolmates and fellow St. Joseph's girls who told me how much my story had meant to them and how proud they were to know me. Women stopped me in the street and said, 'Thank you for being our voice.' It was like nothing I had ever experienced before and it meant a great deal to me. For the first time in my life, I was proud to be 'Majella Moynihan'.

Several former colleagues, whom I knew when we were all of garda rank, apologised to me and said they wished they could have done more for me at the time. As it happened, those messages came from people whom I felt had done the best they could. I hold those gardaí and ex-gardaí in the very highest esteem.

Epilogue

After leaving the guards, I went back to college and studied anatomy and physiology, Indian head massage, holistic massage, integrated energy therapy and reiki. I know from personal experience the wonderful benefits of those treatments and I am certain that they have kept me alive. My days are now spent helping others to heal and it has brought meaning and joy to my life.

As far as things stand with David, it is a difficult situation for both of us. It has always felt to me as though my baby was taken away and after twenty-seven years a man appeared. Although the relationship is a complex one, which I know will require a lot of work and mutual understanding to develop into what we might like it to be, I will always long for a close bond with my son – a man for whom I have the deepest admiration and love.

I am still in receipt of a half-pension from An Garda Síochána. After meeting with the garda commissioner and the minister for justice, I believed that my proceedings would be dealt with promptly but unfortunately this has not been the case. I look forward to the closure that I know one day will come.

Although my marriage to Martin sadly broke down in recent years, our beautiful son Stephen will always be the centre of my world.

I am grateful to have had the opportunity to tell my story. Setting it out in writing has not been easy, raking through years of painful memories to eke out understanding, perspective, meaning. It doesn't always come. There are things I know I will never understand, or accept. There are wounds I know cannot be fully healed. But that, in itself, is an acceptance, making pain all the more tolerable.

Telling my story in my own words has been a healing journey. It forced me out of my comfort zone, to reassess myself, my working life, my *value*. I emerge from it with renewed self-knowledge – of my authentic self, not the doubting, pained, diminished self that prevailed for so much of my life.

It has been an act of walking back through time's dark maze and finding at its earliest beginning a small child, sad and lonely; of taking her into my embrace;

of telling her she is loved, valued, cherished; of placing her in my heart and resolving that, no matter what, I am her guardian and I will always protect her. After all, only we know what we have been through.

This act of self-reclamation has given me a new lease of life and the freedom to move forward. I know that I will embrace every new challenge that comes my way. I can hold my own with anyone now and, for that awakening, I am eternally grateful.

Acknowledgements

A very special thanks to Aoife Kelleher, my wonderful ghost-writer – I could not have done this without you – and to my publisher and editor Ciara Considine for all her guidance and support throughout the process. To Breda Purdue, Elaine Egan and all at Hachette Books Ireland.

To my friends, heartfelt thanks for all your support: Liz O'Callaghan, Carmel McDonnell Byrne, Edel Higgins, Anne Higgins, Annette Flynn, Laura Elliott, Mary Corkery, Ciara O'Keeffe, Nora Barry, Deirdre Ryan, Carol Ward, Catherine Moran, Sr. Noreen O'Connor and Eileen Deane.